SOR JUANA INES DE LA CRUZ
POEMS

A BILINGUAL ANTHOLOGY

Bilingual Press/Editorial Bilingüe

General Editor
    Gary D. Keller

Managing Editor
    Karen S. Van Hooft

Associate Editors
    Karen M. Akins
    Barbara H. Firoozye

Assistant Editor
    Linda St. George Thurston

Editorial Board
    Juan Goytisolo
    Francisco Jiménez
    Eduardo Rivera
    Mario Vargas Llosa

Address:
Bilingual Press
Hispanic Research Center
Arizona State University
P.O. Box 872702
Tempe, Arizona 85287-2702
(602) 965-3867

Sor Juana Inés de la Cruz Poems

Translated from the Spanish by
Margaret Sayers Peden

Bilingual Press/Editorial Bilingüe
Tempe, Arizona

This book is for the four:
Kyle, Kerry, Sally, and Eliza,
and, of course and as always,
for Bill.

ISBN: 0-916950-60-3

Library of Congress Catalog Card Number: 85-71537

Printed in the United States of America

Cover design by Christopher J. Bidlack
Text design by Hillside Studio
Cover photograph by Gabriel North Seymour, from
A Woman of Genius: The Intellectual Autobiography
of Sor Juana Inés de la Cruz, *published by Lime Rock*
Press, Inc., Salisbury, Connecticut 06068

Acknowledgments

I want to express my gratitude to
the Rockefeller Foundation for
my residency at their Study and
Conference Center in Bellagio, Italy,
where many of these poems were
translated. I also want to thank the
following journals for permission to
reprint translations originally published
in their pages: *Nimrod*, epigram 95,
sonnets 145, 164, and 165 (Spring/
Summer 1983); *River Styx 13* epigrams
93 and 97 (1983), and *River Styx 15*,
romance 92 (1984); *Chasqui 12*,
monologue from *Los empeños de una
casa* (1982); and *New Letters*, *décimas*
113 and 130 (1984); as well as John
Bierhorst for his permission to include
his translation from the Nahuatl. I am
grateful to Magdalena García Pinto and
Daniel Gulstad for their frequent and
welcome assistance. Finally, my thanks
to Ed King for his invaluable advice.

Contents

Introduction, 1

Romances, 11

> Prologue to the Reader, 13
> In Reply to a Gentleman from Peru, 17
> While by Grace, 25

Redondillas, 27

> A Philosophical Satire, 29

Epigrams, 35

> Satiric Reproach, 37
> Which Reveals, 37
> A Much-Needed Eyewash, 39
> A Bit of Moral Advice, 39
> Demonstration to a Sergeant, 41

Décimas, 43

> She Assures That She Will Hold a Secret, 45
> Accompanying a Ring, 45
> A Modest Gift, 47
> She Describes in Detail, 47

Sonnets, 49

> She Attempts to Minimize the Praise, 51
> She Laments Her Fortune, 53
> Better Death, 55

Spiritedly, She Considers the Choice, 57
She Distrusts, as Disguised Cruelty, 59
One of Five Burlesque Sonnets, 61
She Answers Suspicions, 63
She Recounts How Fantasy Contents Itself, 65
She Resolves the Question, 67

Silvas, 69

Fragment from *Primero sueño*, 71

Villancicos, 79

Tocotín, 81
Fragment from "Santa Catarina," 83

Theater, Sacred and Profane, 87

Loa for "El Divino Narciso," 89
Fragment from "Los empeños de una casa," 129

Notes, 134

Introduction

This collection of translations of the poetry of Sor Juana Inés de la Cruz grows out of a love affair with the poetry of that seventeenth century nun and of a fascination with her vital personality.

In 1691 Sor Juana, beseiged by a church hierarchy demanding that she renounce her worldly writing, composed the "Respuesta a Sor Filotea" [Response to Sor Filotea], the first document in our hemisphere to defend a woman's right to teach, to study, and to write. As an intellectual woman in a world in which male dominance and, especially, ecclesiastical male dominance, was the rule, Sor Juana's art, her beauty, and her spirit led her inexorably toward the confrontation that produced the "Respuesta." That passionate yet icily rational outburst was followed by four years of nearly total silence. She acceded to the insistent demands of the Church hierarchy; she surrendered her books and her collections of musical and mathematical instruments; she ended her communication with the world of the Viceregal court; she reaffirmed her vows to the Church, signing at least two documents in her own blood; and in 1695, during a devastating plague in which all evidence confirms her heroic devotion to her stricken sisters, she died.

It is possible to document only a few of the major events of Sor Juana's life. About the details of that life, the ordinary, day-to-day activities, we can only conjecture. Sor Juana's voluminous correspondence is lost. The greatest part of convent and church records were destroyed in the anti-clerical fervor of the Mexican Revolution. Of her childhood in Nepantla, of the years as a young girl spent with relatives in Mexico City, of the all-important years of adolescence and young womanhood spent in the heady atmosphere of the Viceregal Court of New Spain, we know almost nothing.

Even three centuries after Sor Juana's birth, two almost contemporaneous documents remain as the principal sources for biographical information: the "Respuesta" itself, and the imprimatur—more a biographical eulogy than a *nihil obstat*—issued by the Spanish priest Diego Calleja on the occasion of the publication of Sor Juana's *Fama y Obras Póstumas* (Madrid, 1700). During the two centuries following her death, the baroque in general and Sor Juana's work in particular were relegated to the realm of bad taste. The German Romantics are generally credited with reawakening interest in the Spanish baroque, a reevaluation that opened the way to a reconsideration of Sor Juana's writing and, slightly later, to biographical research. In our own century, investigation by a handful of Sor Juanistas—among them, Dorothy Schons, Guillermo Ramírez España, and Enrique A. Cervantes—unearthed a handful of legal and church records pertaining to Sor Juana's life and family history. Beyond the information contained in these documents, some of which is questionable and some obviously in error (particularly the well-intentioned but often historically inaccurate account by Padre Calleja), scholars have been forced to, and seduced into, speculation and conjecture in order to flesh out a "portrait" of the intriguing *Décima musa* [Tenth Muse]. As might be expected, such conjecture has resulted in amazing extremes of interpretation: Sor Juana was a true mystic; Sor Juana was a scheming hypocrite who artfully duped the Inquisition; Sor Juana became a nun because she was rejected by a lover; Sor Juana was a narcissist with strongly masculine tendencies; Sor Juana's tragedy was to have been born a woman; Sor Juana's greatness was the gentleness of a feminine heart.

Much of this psychological speculation and biographical irresponsiblity has recently been countered in a book by Octavio Paz, *Sor Juana Inés de la Cruz o Las Trampas de la Fe.* Paz's study is unlikely to be surpassed until and unless substantial new documentation comes to light. *Sor Juana Inés de la Cruz. . .* combines a new vision of Mexican colonial history, the most reasoned interpretation to date of the Sor Juana biographical materials, and brilliant literary criticism. For anyone interested in Sor Juana, in the baroque, in the colonial period, in poetry in general, *Sor Juana Inés de la Cruz. . .* is an indispensable reference.

Briefly, the facts about Sor Juana's life are the following, although we must begin with some uncertainty. For over two centuries scholars accepted Padre Calleja's evidence and Sor Juana's own testimony, as well as inscriptions on nearly contemporaneous portraits, establishing her date of birth as 1651. That date was questioned, however, by the discovery of an entry in a church registry that seems to establish Sor Juana's birth as December 2, 1648. The reasons for the discrepancy are unclear, but probably were influenced by Sor Juana's desire to confirm her legitimacy by obscuring her true date of birth. The registry entry is for a girl child "Inés, daughter of the Church," a term used when recording an illegitimate birth. That legitimacy would not have been of supreme importance in Sor Juana's time, except for the accident of her genius, which led her to the highest social circles of New Spain, where the question of birth may have borne on her eligibility for a good marriage and her entry into the convent of San Jerónimo.

Sor Juana lived in Nepantla, the tiny village of her birth, either five or eight years, depending which birth date one accepts. While she probably did not know her father, the influence of her grandfather, a man with a considerable library and three remarkably independent daughters, is widely acknowledged. It is known that in the year of his death, 1656, Sor Juana was sent to Mexico City to live with her well-to-do aunt and uncle. Among the most famous and most touching passages in the "Respuesta" are those recounting incidents in her early life. Sor Juana tells of following her sister to school, of learning to read there unbeknownst to her mother, "inflamed by the desire to know how to read." She tells of abstaining from eating cheese because she had heard "that it made one slow of wits" and that in her "the desire for learning was stronger than the desire for eating." When, quoting Sor Juana, she was "six or seven," she heard that there was a University in Mexico City "in which one studied the sciences" (i.e., all learning). She begged her mother to dress her in boy's clothing, "to study and be tutored at the University," and of course was refused. Once in Mexico City, Sor Juana learned Latin in twenty lessons. She writes that in spite of the high esteem in which young ladies held the "adornment" of hair, she cut off her own if she had not learned "such and such a thing" she had set for herself to learn, as "punishment for being so slow-witted," believing that "there was no cause for a head to be adorned with hair and naked of learning."

We know virtually nothing about the years that Juana Inés lived with her relatives, the Matas, in Mexico City. We do know that word of Sor Juana's unusual intelligence and learning spread rapidly. Calleja records how Don Antonio Sebastián de Toledo, Marqués de Mancera and Viceroy of New Spain, called together the most learned men in the land—forty theologians, philosophers, mathematicians, historians, poets, and humanists—to examine the young woman of whom everyone was talking. The Viceroy reported to Calleja "that in the manner that a royal galleon might fend off the attacks of small canoes, so did Juana extricate herself from the questions, arguments, and objections these many men, each in his speciality, directed to her." In addition, Sor Juana quickly won the affection of the Vicereine, and spent two years in the Viceregal Palace as her protegée. Those vitally important years probably constitute the most serious lacuna in reconstructing the poet's life, and must be derived from her writing.

In 1667, for reasons that have not been ascertained, Sor Juana entered the convent of the Carmelitas Descalzas. Whether for reasons of health—as Méndez Plancarte, the editor of her *Obras completas* believes—or because the rules of the order were too strict for her tastes—as others have argued—she remained only three months with the Carmelites. In 1669, however, Sor Juana made her definite decision and entered the convent of San Jerónimo, where she studied and wrote until the crisis of the "Respuesta" in 1691, and where she lived until her death in 1695.

Sor Juana's life in the convent, while not documented in detail, can be deduced in some degree—as Méndez Plancarte has done by his ordering and classifying of her work in the *Obras completas*. Among the most significant influences of those years—and more years of her life were spent inside than outside the convent—were her human relationships. Sor Juana may have separated herself physically from the

Viceregal Palace but she did not abandon her contacts there. Don Tomás Antonio de la Cerda, Marqués de la Laguna, succeeded the Marqués de Mancera as Viceroy. María Luisa Manrique de Lara y Gonzaga, his Vicereine, succeeded the Marquesa de Mancera, Leonor Carreto, and her patronage was as fervent as that of her predecessor. Poems and gifts flowed between palace and convent. In fact, a major portion of Sor Juana's poems were written to celebrate some event in courtly life: a birth, a death, the arrival of a new representative of Spanish rule. Sor Juana also shared friendships with the leading intellectuals of both continents, and one of the true misfortunes for the study of her times, as well as of her own life, is the loss of that correspondence.

Of one thing we can be sure. Sor Juana was the target of envy and jealousy throughout her adult life. Those themes occur again and again in her poems, and are a major concern in the "Respuesta." The injunctions of the Church, the demands that she devote herself more exclusively to religious duties and put away worldly things, seem to have been occasioned as much by jealousy as by true concern for her salvation. We can agree that her downfall—for most commentators agree that the crisis of the "Respuesta" was tantamount to a kind of death—was caused, as in most tragedies, by human frailties. And it may be argued that to some degree Sor Juana was destroyed by her own ambition and pride. But all must agree that she was the victim of the jealousy and wrath of powerful individuals in her society, as well as of that society itself, a society incapable of allowing her genius normal expression.

It is difficult to understand how a woman of such genius has remained in almost total obscurity in the English-speaking world. Sor Juana is unarguably the finest poet of the Latin American baroque period, and Carlos Fuentes has called her "Latin America's greatest poet." She is personally compelling: contemporary Latin writers dedicate plays to her and write poems about her. The enigmatic gaze from one of Sor Juana's best-known portraits adorns the Mexican thousand peso note, a very visible icon. Perhaps the answer to her *in*visibility in our own world lies deep within the labyrinthine complexities of the baroque. The language of the baroque can be tortured. Its forms are strict. Its concepts and conceits are based in antithesis. The allusions are so literary as to suggest pedantry. These are not our literary styles, not our language, not our forms. And those styles, that language, those forms are but the signs of the society they represent. Sor Juana's world was rigid, strict, tortured, pedantic—baroque. The eighteenth and nineteenth centuries found that world and her writing incomprehensible. The twentieth? While its sensibilities are in many superifical ways the opposite to our own, it is obvious that there are resonances in the baroque, perhaps in its world vision, that make us once again receptive to that literary period. Whatever the reasons, it is clear that Sor Juana has been rediscovered, revindicated, re-enshrined in the Latin world. Paz's book alone is witness to that truth. And for the first time, it seems possible that the figure and the poetry of Sor Juana Inés de la Cruz will begin to find their place in the consciousness of an English-speaking public. While articles of general interest about Sor Juana and translations of her work published in English prior to 1980 are extremely limited, work in progress (the translation of the Paz study and various translations of her poetry) will rapidly expand the availability of materials for an English-language audience. In the scholarly community, a bibliography of articles written in Spanish would fill a book, while articles in English are almost nonexistent. It is almost as if the circle of Sor Juana critics and devotées had turned their backs to English speakers, subconsciously gauging their indifference. This, too, is beginning to change. It appears that Sor Juana's hour has come.

To return to the reasons for this collection, and to turn to the personal, I would like to address the motivation for this undoubtedly eccentric selection of poems taken from among the over two hundred individual poems and enormous body of songs, devotional exercises, and plays written in verse. I don't remember the first poem I translated. I know that I had first translated her famous "Respuesta a Sor Filotea," and it is only in looking back that I can see a pattern in the poetry selections. I believe that each of the poems I chose to translate in some way reveals something of Sor Juana, even though that something might not be immediately apparent. The desire to enter into her mind through her writing, to know the woman through the work, obviously explains the choice of such generally acknowledged autobiographical pieces as the sonnet to her portrait (145) and the fragment of Doña Leonor's monologue from "Los empeños de una casa" (386); this is also, however, the rationale for including less discussed but still surely autobiographical pieces like the prologue to the second edition of her first published collection (1), the reply to the "Gentleman from Peru" (48), and the stunning sonnet in which she laments "a state enduring unto Death" (149). The "Philosophical Satire" (92) that is her single most widely anthologized poem overtly expresses opinions and attitudes that may be more subtly echoed in the vapid, if technically perfect, Fabio/Silvio love poems, one of which is represented here (166), or even contradicted in poems that seem to speak of real and experienced pain (sonnets 164 and 165). What is one to make of the burlesque and ribald games of her five burlesque sonnets, only one of which appears here (161, III)? I believe that they are one aspect of a sense of playfulness that is expressed in many of her poems but seldom discussed in any assessment of her character; this is the same playfulness that instructs her reader (in the previously mentioned prologue) not to unroll the entire bolt if he doesn't like the sample, and reaches truly humorous expression in the cliché-ridden *décima* describing Fili (132), whose foot is so tiny it cannot even fill a line of poetry.

Some of Sor Juana's poems, *many* of Sor Juana's poems, were commissioned, a fact that dictates caution when claiming, as I am, that something of Sor Juana is revealed in them. I acknowledge that need for caution, but I must believe that the *villancico* dedicated to Saint Catherine (317) reveals Sor Juana's sense of identification with that Alexandrian saint who represented learning as well as martyrdom. While the other *décimas* (113, 126, and 130) I have included in addition to the one extolling Fili's virtues reveal a Sor Juana whose intimate moments—guarding a secret, giving a gift—are characterized by tenderness, warmth, and wit, the five epigrams I have translated (93–97), the only five she wrote, suggest an entirely different Sor Juana, one in whom wit has turned to savage satire, and tenderness curdled into vitriol. Yet these poems are more than a curiosity, in my view; they support a reading of the "Respuesta" that many critics have denied. How can one read the devastating epigram about "Dear Leonor" and not hear the icily controlled rage, the rapier thrust of irony in the subtext of the "Respuesta," the quality that makes that document a protest rather than a submission?

The longest piece in this collection, as well as the charming *tocotín* written in Nahuatl (224), represent an aspect of Sor Juana's writing that has not received sufficient attention. Sor Juana was surely one of the first native-born Americans to defend the peoples and the customs of our hemisphere. One thinks of the early chroniclers of the Conquest, who described the New World with awe and amazement, and of a literary figure like the Inca Garcilaso, who was among the first to introduce American legends and myths to Europeans. But where in literature before Sor Juana did one find characters speaking such astounding lines as these:

> AMERICA . . . for though my person come to harm,
> and though I weep for liberty,
> my liberty of will, will grow,
> and I shall still adore my Gods!

or these:

> OCCIDENT . . . though captive I may moan in pain,
> your will can never conquer mine,
> and in my heart I will proclaim:
> I worship the great God of Seeds!

It is true that ultimately AMERICA and OCCIDENT are converted to the True Faith. The lines, nevertheless, stand as testimony to a kind of fierce defensíveness of the rights and virtues of the New World that may have as its analogue a subconscious defense of her own condition.

The *Primero sueño* is the Mount Everest of Sor Juana's writing. It is her masterpiece, and one must attempt to scale it simply because it is there. I have attempted only an exploratory climb. I shall return to it some day.

Finally, I would like to add a comment about my philosophy in making these translations. In *After Babel* George Steiner accurately depicts the act of translation as "a transparent absurdity, an endeavor to go backwards up the escalator of time." "Art dies," he says, "when we lose or ignore the conventions by which it can be read." He suggests that in rereading the baroque, we must extend the "backward reach of our senses." I have experienced the weight of this truth. The baroque cannot come to us. We must go to the baroque; we must attempt to recreate it by means of that backward reach. This is the reason why I have chosen to translate these poems with meter and with verse. Sor Juana's world, her very reality, is represented in the strict hierarchy of her forms and the elegance of her rhetoric. With few exceptions—the most notable, perhaps, the epigrams—I cannot conceive of those forms and that rhetoric being expressed in the unstructured lines or conversational language of much contemporary poetry. While I am obviously not capable of perfectly recreating Sor Juana's verse, I believe that the greater service is to make the attempt within the conceptual frameworks of her art.

May passion serve as apology for imperfection.

Romances

Octasyllabic lines with second
and fourth lines in assonant rhyme

Prólogo al lector

Estos Versos, lector mío,
que a tu deleite consagro,
y sólo tienen de buenos
conocer yo que son malos,
   ni disputártelos quiero
ni quiero recomendarlos,
porque eso fuera querer
hacer de ellos mucho caso.
   No agradecido te busco:
pues no debes, bien mirado,
estimar lo que yo nunca
juzgué que fuera a tus manos.
   En tu libertad te pongo,
si quisieres censurarlos;
pues de que, al cabo, te estás
en ella, estoy muy al cabo.
   No hay cosa más libre que
el entendimiento humano;
¿pues lo que Dios no violenta,
por qué yo he de violentarlo?
   Di cuanto quisieres de ellos,
que, cuando más inhumano
me los mordieres, entonces
me quedas más obligado,
   pues le debes a mi Musa
el más sazonado plato
(que es el murmurar), según
un adagio cortesano.
   Y siempre te sirvo, pues
o te agrado, o no te agrado:
si te agrado, te diviertes;
murmuras, si no te cuadro.
   Bien pudiera yo decirte
por disculpa, que no ha dado
lugar para corregirlos
la prisa de los traslados;

Prologue to the Reader

These poems, Dear Reader, I give you
with hopes your pleasure they ensure,
though all that may speak well of them
is that I know them to be poor;
      I do not wish to argue them,
nor of their worth give evidence,
for such attention to these lines
would seem to lend them consequence.
      Nor do I seek your good esteem,
for, after all, no one demands
you value what I never thought
would find its way into your hands.
      If you should wish to criticize,
I place you in full liberty,
as I am free now to conclude,
you may conclude that you are free.
      We know nothing as unbound
as our human intellect;
and what God never violates,
should I not honor and respect?
      Say of these verses what you will,
the more that you are inhumane,
and at them cruelly bite and gnaw,
the more my debtor you remain,
      for in the Court it is well known
that only through my Muse's grace
do you enjoy that richest dish,
the spiteful chatter you embrace.
      How well I serve you, at all times,
in pleasing you or pleasing not;
you are diverted if I please,
and gossip if I come to naught.
      In asking pardon, I might say
I hoped some poems to remedy,
but due to haste in copying,
had little opportunity;

que van de diversas letras,
y que algunas, de muchachos,
matan de suerte el sentido
que es cadáver el vocablo;

  y que, cuando los he hecho,
ha sido en el corto espacio
que ferian al ocio las
precisiones de mi estado;

  que tengo poca salud
y continuos embarazos,
tales, que aun diciendo esto,
llevo la pluma trotando.

  Pero todo eso no sirve,
pues pensarás que me jacto
de que quizás fueran buenos
a haberlos hecho despacio;

  y no quiero que tal creas,
sino sólo que es el darlos
a la luz, tan sólo por
obedecer un mandato.

  Esto es, si gustas creerlo,
que sobre eso no me mato,
pues al cabo harás lo que
se te pusiere en los cascos.

  Y a Dios, que esto no es más de
darte la muestra del paño:
si no te agrada la pieza,
no desenvuelvas el fardo.

they come in many different hands
and some, where little lads have erred,
do kill the sense, and you will see
cadavers made of living words,
    besides which, when I wrote these lines,
they were composed in those rare fêtes
when leisure called a holiday
amidst the duties of my state;
    for I suffer from ill-health,
my life, with obstacles is fraught,
so many, even as I write,
my pen is racing at a trot.
    But pay no heed to what I say,
lest you think I vaunt my rhymes,
suggesting that they would be good
had I but had sufficient time;
    I would not have you so believe,
for their life, their existence,
the cause for bringing them to light,
was dutiful obedience.
    And so it is, think as you will,
I do not die to have them read,
and you are free to do with them
whatever comes into your head.
    Godspeed to you, all I do here
is show a piece, but not the whole:
so if you do not like the cloth,
the bolt were better left unrolled.

48

Respondiendo a un Caballero del Perú, que le envió unos Barros diciéndole que se volviese hombre

Señor: para responderos
todas las Musas se eximen,
sin que haya, ni aun de limosna,
una que ahora me dicte;
     y siendo las nueve Hermanas
madres del donaire y chiste,
no hay, oyendo vuestros versos,
una que chiste ni miste.

Apolo absorto se queda
tan elevado de oírle,
que para aguijar el Carro,
es menester que le griten.

     Para escucharlo, el Pegaso
todo el aliento reprime,
sin que mientras lo recitan
tema nadie que relinche.

     Pára, contra todo el orden,
de sus cristales fluxibles
los gorjeos Helicona,
los murmurios Aganipe:

     porque sus murmurios viendo,
todas las Musas coligen
que, de vuestros versos, no
merecen ser aprendices.

     Apolo suelta la vara
con que los compases rige,
porque reconoce, al veros,
que injustamente preside.

     Y así, el responderos tengo
del todo por imposible,
si compadecido acaso
vos no tratáis de inflüirme.

48

In Reply to a Gentleman from Peru,
Who Sent Her Clay Vessels While Suggesting
She Would Better Be a Man

    Kind Sir, while wishing to reply,
my Muses all have taken leave,
and none, even for charity,
will aid me now I wish to speak;
    and though we know these Sisters nine
good mothers are of wit and jest,
not one, once having heard your verse,
will dare to jest at my behest.
    The God Apollo listens, rapt,
and races on, so high aloft
that those who guide his Chariot
must raise their voices to a shout.
    To hear your lines, fleet Pegasus
his lusty breathing will retain,
that no one fear his thunderous neigh
as your verses are declaimed.
    Checking, against nature's order,
altering crystalline watercourse,
Helicon stays its gurgling water,
Agannipe, her murmuring source:
    for, having heard your murmuring,
the Nine Daughters all concede,
beside your verses they are wanting,
unfit to study at your feet.
    Apollo sets aside the wand
that he employs to mark the beat,
because, on seeing you, he knows
he cannot justly take the lead.
    And thus, acknowledge it I must,
I cannot scribe the verses owed
unless, perhaps, compassionate,
keen inspiration you bestow.

Sed mi Apolo, y veréis que
(como vuestra luz me anime)
mi lira sonante escuchan
los dos opuestos confines.

Mas ¡oh cuánto poderosa
es la invocación humilde,
pues ya, en nuevo aliento, el pecho
nuevo espíritu concibe!

De extraño ardor inflamado,
hace que incendios respire;
y como de Apolo, de
Navarrete se reviste.

Nuevas sendas al discurso
hace, que elevado pise,
y en nuevos conceptos hace
que él a sí mismo se admire.

Balbuciente con la copia,
la lengua torpe se aflige:
mucho ve, y explica poco;
mucho entiende, y poco dice.

Pensaréis que estoy burlando;
pues mirad, que el que me asiste
espíritu, no está a un
dedo de que profetice.

Mas si es querer alabaros
tan reservado imposible,
que en vuestra pluma, no más,
puede parecer factible,

¿de qué me sirve emprenderlo,
de qué intentarlo me sirve,
habiendo plumas que en agua
sus escarmientos escriben?

Dejo ya vuestros elogios
a que ellos solos se expliquen:
pues los que en sí sólo caben,
consigo sólo se miden.

Be my Apollo, and behold
(as your light illumines me)
how my lyre will then be heard
the length and breadth of land and sea.

Though humble, oh, how powerful
my invocation's consequence,
I find new valor in my breast,
new spirit given utterance!

Ignited with unfamiliar fervor,
my pen bursting into flame,
while giving due to famed Apollo
I honor Navarrete's name.

Traveling where none has trod,
expression rises to new heights,
and, reveling in new invention,
finds in itself supreme delight.

Stammering with such abundance
my clumsy tongue is tied with pain:
much is seen, but little spoken,
some is known, but none explained.

You will think that I make mock;
no, nothing further from the truth,
to prophesy, my guiding spirit
is lacking but a fine hair's breadth.

But if I am so little able
to offer you sufficient praise,
to form the kind of compliment
that only your apt pen may phrase,

what serve me then to undertake it?
to venture it, what good will serve?
if mine be pens that write in water,
recording lessons unobserved.

That they themselves elucidate,
I now leave your eulogies:
as none to their measure correspond,
none can match them in degree,

Y paso a estimar aquellos
hermosamente sutiles
Búcaros, en quien el Arte
hace al apetito brindis:

Barros en cuyo primor
ostenta soberbio Chile,
que no es la plata, no el oro,
lo que tiene más plausible,

pues por tan baja materia
hace que se desestimen
doradas Copas que néctar
en sagradas mesas sirven.

Bésoos las manos por ellos,
que es cierto que tanto filis
tienen los Barros, que juzgo
que sois vos quien los hicisteis.

Y en el consejo que dais,
yo os prometo recibirle
y hacerme fuerza, aunque juzgo
que no hay fuerzas que entarquinen:

porque acá Sálmacis falta,
en cuyos cristales dicen
que hay no sé qué virtud de
dar alientos varoniles.

Yo no entiendo de esas cosas;
sólo sé que aquí me vine
porque, si es que soy mujer,
ninguno lo verifique.

Y también sé que, en latín,
sólo a las casadas dicen
úxor, o mujer, y que
es común de dos lo Virgen.

Con que a mí no es bien mirado
que como a mujer me miren,
pues no soy mujer que a alguno
de mujer pueda servirle;

and I turn to giving thanks
for your fair gifts, most subtly made;
Art lifts a toast to appetite
in lovely Vessels of fragrant clay.

Earthenware, so exquisite
that Chile properly is proud,
though it is not gold or silver
that gives your gift its wide renown

but, rather, from such lowly matter
forms emerge that put to shame
the brimming Goblets made of gold
from which the Gods their nectar drained.

Kiss, I beg, the hands that made them,
though judging by the Vessels' charm
—such grace can surely leave no doubt—
yours were the hands that gave them form.

As for the counsel that you offer,
I promise you, I will attend
with all my strength, although I judge
no strength on earth can en-Tarquin:

for here we have no Salmacis,
whose crystal water, so they tell,
to nurture masculinity
possesses powers unexcelled.

I have no knowledge of these things,
except that I came to this place
so that, if true that I am female,
none substantiate that state.

I know, too, that they were wont
to call wife, or woman, in the Latin
uxor, only those who wed,
though wife or woman might be virgin.

So in my case, it is not seemly
that I be viewed as feminine,
as I will never be a woman
who may as woman serve a man.

y sólo sé que mi cuerpo,
sin que a uno u otro se incline,
es neutro, o abstracto, cuanto
sólo el Alma deposite.

Y dejando esta cuestión
para que otros la ventilen,
porque en lo que es bien que ignore,
no es razón que sutilice

generoso Perüano
que os lamentáis de infelice,
¿que Lima es la que dejasteis,
si acá la *lima* os trajisteis?

Bien sabéis la ley de Atenas,
con que desterró a Aristides:
que aun en lo bueno, es delito
el que se singularice.

Por bueno lo desterraron,
y a otros varones insignes;
porque el exceder a todos,
es delito irremisible.

El que a todos se aventaja,
fuerza es que a todos incite
a envidia, pues él lucir
a todos juntos impide.

Al paso que la alabanza
a uno para blanco elige,
a ese mismo paso trata
la envidia de perseguirle.

A vos de Perú os destierran
y nuestra Patria os admite,
porque nos da el Cielo acá
la dicha que allá despiden.

Bien es que vuestro talento
diversos climas habite:
que los que nacen tan grandes,
no sólo para sí viven.

I know only that my body,
not to either state inclined,
is neuter, abstract, guardian
of only what my Soul consigns.

Let us renounce this argument,
let others, if they will, debate;
some matters better left unknown
no reason can illuminate.

Generous gentleman from Peru,
proclaiming such unhappiness,
did you leave Lima any art,
given the art you brought to us?

You must know that law of Athens
by which Aristides was expelled:
it seems that, even if for good,
it is forbidden to excel.

He was expelled for being good,
and other famous men as well;
because to tower over all
is truly unforgiveable.

He who always leads his peers
will by necessity invite
malicious envy, as his fame
will rob all others of the light.

To the degree that one is chosen
as the target for acclaim,
to that same measure, envy trails
in close pursuit, with perfect aim.

Now you are banished from Peru
and welcomed in my Native Land,
we see the Heavens grant to us
the blessing that Peru declined.

But it is well that such great talent
live in many different zones,
for those who are with greatness born
should live not for themselves alone.

Mientras la Gracia me excita
por elevarme a la Esfera,
más me abate a lo profundo
el peso de mis miserias.

La virtud y la costumbre
en el corazón pelean,
y el corazón agoniza
en tanto que lidian ellas.

Y aunque es la virtud tan fuerte,
temo que tal vez la venzan,
que es muy grande la costumbre
y está la virtud muy tierna.

Obscurécese el discurso
entre confusas tinieblas;
pues ¿quién podrá darme luz
si está la razón a ciegas?

De mí mesma soy verdugo
y soy cárcel de mí mesma.
¿Quién vio que pena y penante
una propia cosa sean?

Hago disgusto a lo mismo
que más agradar quisiera;
y del disgusto que doy,
en mí resulta la pena.

Amo a Dios y siento en Dios;
y hace mi voluntad mesma
de lo que es alivio, cruz,
del mismo puerto, tormenta.

Padezca, pues Dios lo manda;
mas de tal manera sea,
que si son penas las culpas,
que no sean culpas las penas.

  While by Grace I am inspired,
'tis then I near the precipice,
I would ascend unto the Sphere,
but am dragged down to the abyss.

  Virtue and custom are at odds,
and deep within my heart contend,
my anguished heart will agonize
until the two their combat end.

  I fear that virtue will be crushed,
though all know its just repute,
for custom is long flourishing,
and virtue, tender as a shoot.

  My thinking often is obscured,
among dark shadows ill-defined,
then who is there to give me light,
when reason falters as if blind?

  Of myself I am the gaoler,
I, executioner of me,
who can know the painful pain,
who can know the tragedy?

  I cause displeasure to the One
I most desire to gratify,
and from displeasure that I give,
the one who suffers most is I.

  I love and find myself in God,
but my will His grace transforms,
turning solace to a cross,
quitting port to seek the storm.

  Then suffer, it is God's command,
but let this be the paradigm,
that though your sins cause suffering,
your suffering not be seen as sin.

Redondillas

Octosyllabic quatrains, usually rhyming *abba*

Sátira filosófica

*Arguye de inconsecuentes el gusto y la censura de los
hombres que en las mujeres acusan lo que causan.*

Hombres necios que acusáis
a la mujer sin razón,
sin ver que sois la ocasión
de lo mismo que culpáis:

si con ansia sin igual
solicitáis su desdén,
¿por qué queréis que obren bien
si las incitáis al mal?

Combatís su resistencia
y luego, con gravedad,
decís que fue liviandad
lo que hizo la diligencia.

Parecer quiere el denuedo
de vuestro parecer loco,
al niño que pone el coco
y luego le tiene miedo.

Queréis, con presunción necia,
hallar a la que buscáis,
para prentendida, Thais,
y en la posesión, Lucrecia.

¿Qué humor puede ser más raro
que el que, falto de consejo,
él mismo empaña el espejo,
y siente que no esté claro?

A Philosophical Satire

She proves the inconsistency of the caprice and criticism
of men who accuse women of what they cause

> Misguided men, who will chastize
> a woman when no blame is due,
> oblivious that it is you
> who prompted what you criticize;
>   if your passions are so strong
> that you elicit their disdain,
> how can you wish that they refrain
> when you incite them to do wrong?
>   You strive to topple their defense,
> and then, with utmost gravity,
> you credit sensuality
> for what was won with diligence.
>   Your daring must be qualified,
> your sense is no less senseless than
> the child who calls the boogeyman,
> then weeps when he is terrified.
>   Your mad presumption knows no bounds,
> though for a wife you want Lucrece,
> in lovers you prefer Thaïs,
> thus seeking blessings to compound.
>   If knowingly one clouds a mirror
> —was ever humor so absurd
> or good counsel so obscured?—
> can he lament it is not clearer?

Con el favor y el desdén
tenéis condición igual,
quejándoos, si os tratan mal,
burlándoos, si os quieren bien.

Opinión, ninguna gana;
pues la que más se recata,
si no os admite, es ingrata,
y si os admite, es liviana.

Siempre tan necios andáis
que, con desigual nivel,
a una culpáis por crüel
y a otra por fácil culpáis.

¿Pues cómo ha de estar templada
la que vuestro amor pretende,
si la que es ingrata, ofende,
y la que es fácil, enfada?

Mas, entre el enfado y pena
que vuestro gusto refiere,
bien haya la que no os quiere
y quejaos en hora buena.

Dan vuestra amantes penas
a sus libertades alas,
y después de hacerlas malas
las queréis hallar muy buenas.

¿Cuál mayor culpa ha tenido
en una pasión errada:
la que cae de rogada,
o el que ruega de caído?

¿O cuál es más de culpar,
aunque cualquiera mal haga:
la que peca por la paga,
o el que paga por pecar?

Pues ¿para qué os espantáis
de la culpa que tenéis?
Queredlas cual las hacéis
o hacedlas cual las buscáis.

From either favor or disdain
the selfsame purpose you achieve,
if they love, they are deceived,
if they love not, hear you complain.

There is no woman suits your taste,
though circumspection be her virtue:
ungrateful, she who does not love you,
yet she who does, you judge unchaste.

You men are such a foolish breed,
appraising with a faulty rule,
the first you charge with being cruel,
the second, easy, you decree.

So how can she be temperate,
the one who would her love expend?
if not willing, she offends,
but willing, she infuriates.

Amid the anger and torment
your whimsy causes you to bear,
one may be found who does not care:
how quickly then is grievance vent.

So lovingly you inflict pain
that inhibitions fly away;
how, after leading them astray,
can you wish them without stain?

Who does the greater guilt incur
when a passion is misleading?
She who errs and heeds his pleading,
or he who pleads with her to err?

Whose is the greater guilt therein
when either's conduct may dismay:
she who sins and takes the pay,
or he who pays her for the sin?

Why, for sins you're guilty of,
do you, amazed, your blame debate?
Either love what you create
or else create what you can love.

Dejad de solicitar,
y después, con más razón,
acusaréis la afición;
de la que os fuere a rogar.
    Bien con muchas armas fundo
que lidia vuestra arrogancia,
pues en promesa e instancia
juntáis diablo, carne y mundo.

Were not it better to forbear,
and thus, with finer motivation,
obtain the unforced admiration,
of her you plotted to ensnare?
　　But no, I deem you still will revel
in your arms and arrogance,
and in promise and persistence
adjoin flesh and world and devil.

Epigrams

In the Spirit if not the Letter

93

Con un desengaño satírico a una
Presumida de Hermosa

Que te dan en la hermosura
la palma, dices, Leonor;
la de virgen es mejor,
que tu cara la asegura.
    No te precies, con descoco,
que a todos robas el alma:
que si te han dado la Palma,
es, Leonor, porque eres Coco.

94

En que descubre digna estirpe
a un Borracho linajudo

Porque tu sangre se sepa,
cuentas a todos, Alfeo,
que eres de Reyes. Yo creo
que eres de muy buena cepa;
    y que, pues a cuantos topas
con esos Reyes enfadas
que, más que Reyes de Espadas,
debieron de ser de Copas.

93

Satiric Reproach to a Woman Who Boasts of her Beauty

    Dear Leonor, they've given you
the palm for beauty, or so you say,
but have no fear for your virtue,
that face would save you any day.
    You sing your praises without qualm,
to hear you tell it, men lose their wits:
but if they've give you the palm,
it's from the date—for you're the pits.

94

Which Reveals the Honorable Ancestry of a High-Born Drunkard

    Alfeo claims he comes from kings,
he boasts of blood of royal hue,
he speaks of queens with *diamond* rings,
whose *hearts* pump only royal blue.
    The truth is, his line brandished *clubs*,
his House is the House of Topers,
but have no doubt, when in his cups,
he's king—in *spades*—the King of Jokers.

95

Que dan el Colirio merecido a un Soberbio

El no ser de Padre honrado,
fuera defecto, a mi ver,
si como recibí el ser
de él, se lo hubiera yo dado.
　Más piadosa fue tu Madre
que hizo que a muchos sucedas:
para que, entre tantos, puedas
tomar el que más te cuadre.

96

Con advertencia moral, a un Capitán moderno

Capitán es ya Don Juan;
mas quisiera mi cuidado,
hallarle lo reformado
antes de lo Capitán.
　Porque cierto que me inquieta,
en acción tan atrevida,
ver que no sepa la brida
y se atreva a la jineta.

95

A Much-Needed Eyewash for Cleansing the Eyes of an Arrogant Myope

Not to be born of an honorable father
would be a blemish, I must own,
if receiving my being from no other
I did not judge it as his alone.
    Far more generous was your mother
when she arranged your ancestry,
offering many a likely father
among whom to choose your pedigree.

96

A Bit of Moral Advice for a Modern Captain

A Captain now is our Don Juan;
but I would far prefer he serve
by learning tactics of Reserve
before becoming *Capitán*.
    Consider, is he not too cocky,
the man who setting out to ride will,
knowing nothing of the bridle,
spur his mare as if a jockey?

97

*Que demuestran a un Sargento las
circunstancias que le faltan*

De Alabarda vencedora
un tal Sargento se armó;
mas luego él y ella paró
en lo que contaré ahora:
    a ella, una A se desvanece,
porque la *Albarda* suceda;
a él el *Sar*, en *Sarna* queda;
y el *Argento* no parece.

Demonstration to a Sergeant of Ills to Befall

Our Captain Cutlass took up arms one day
and with sword and scabbard set out to the fray;
but to former and latter then befell
the abhorrent fates that now I tell.
When *sword* was *bared* what was left was the *scab*
(to cut*less* from *cutlass* would be just as bad),
with *s* cut from *sword*, the *word's* not the same
and the *sarge* has his *argent*, but only in name.

Décimas

Stanza of ten octosyllabic lines,
usual rhyme scheme, *abbaa/ccddc*

113

*Asegura la confianza de que ocultará
de todo un secreto*

El paje os dirá, discreto,
como, luego que leí,
vuestro secreto rompí
por no romper el secreto.
Y aun hice más, os prometo:
los fragmentos, sin desdén,
del papel, tragué también;
que secretos que venero,
aun en pedazos no quiero
que fuera del pecho estén.

126

*En un Anillo retrató a la Sra.
Condesa de Paredes. Dice por qué*

Este retrato que ha hecho
copiar mi cariño ufano,
es sobrescribir la mano
lo que tiene dentro el pecho:
que, como éste viene estrecho
a tan alta perfección,
brota fuera la afición;
y en el índice la emplea,
para que con verdad sea
índice del corazón.

She Assures That She Will Hold a Secret in Confidence

The page, discreetly, will relate
how, the moment it was read,
I tore your secret into shreds
that shreds be not the secret's fate.
And something more, inviolate,
I swallowed what you had confessed,
the tiny fragments of your note,
to guard the secret that you wrote
and honor thus your confidence, lest
even one scrap escape my breast.

Accompanying a Ring Bearing the Portrait of la Señora Condesa de Paredes. She Explains

This portrait traced by arrogance
was nonetheless by love inspired,
whereon a clumsy hand conspired
to give emotion utterance:
no bursting breast can countenance
for long the presence of perfection,
but needs must spill out its affection;
then let your index finger show
the miniature, that all may know
the ring indexes my subjection.

Presente en que el cariño hace regalo la llaneza

Lysi: a tus manos divinas
doy castañas espinosas,
porque donde sobran rosas
no pueden faltar espinas.
Si a su aspereza te inclinas
y con eso el gusto engañas,
perdona las malas mañas
de quien tal regalo te hizo;
perdona, pues que un erizo
sólo puede dar castañas.

Describe, con énfasis de no poder dar la última mano a la pintura, el retrato de una Belleza

Tersa frente, oro el cabello,
cejas arcos, zafir ojos,
bruñida tez, labios rojos,
nariz recta, ebúrneo cuello;
talle airoso, cuerpo bello,
cándidas manos en que
el cetro de Amor se ve,
tiene Fili; en oro engasta
pie tan breve, que no gasta
ni un pie.

A Modest Gift by Affection Made a Treat

Lysi: into your hands divine
I give two chestnuts with thorny spines,
because where roses bloom in number,
thorns will flowers' stems encumber.
If to their spines you are inclined,
and so contrive to trick your taste,
forgive the shocking lack of grace
of one who sent you such a toy;
for if you would the meats enjoy,
then first you must the burr embrace.

She Describes in Detail—Not to Give the Last Word to Painting—The Portrait of a Beauty

Smooth brow and golden hair,
sapphire eyes and temple fair,
glowing skin, with lips of rose,
ivory throat, a noble nose,
her form is graceful, proud her air;
and in her hands, pale and fine,
see Love's scepter proudly shine:
Fili extolled, with—shod in gold—
a foot so comely it takes only
half a line.

Sonnets

In hendecasyllabic lines and
Italianate rhyme scheme

145

*Procura desmentir los elogios que a un retrato de la
Poetisa inscribió la verdad, que llama pasión*

Este, que ves, engaño colorido,
que del arte ostentando los primores,
con falsos silogismos de colores
es cauteloso engaño del sentido;
    éste, en quien la lisonja ha pretendido
excusar de los años los horrores,
y venciendo del tiempo los rigores
triunfar de la vejez y del olvido,
    es un vano artificio del cuidado,
es una flor al viento delicada,
es un resguardo inútil para el hado:
    es una necia diligencia errada,
es un afán caduco y, bien mirado,
es cádaver, es polvo, es sombra, es nada.

She Attempts to Minimize the Praise Occasioned by a Portrait of Herself Inscribed by Truth—Which She Calls Ardor

This that you gaze on, colorful deceit,
that so immodestly displays art's favors,
with its fallacious arguments of colors
is to the senses cunning counterfeit,
    this on which kindness practiced to delete
from cruel years accumulated horrors,
constraining time to mitigate its rigors,
and thus oblivion and age defeat,
    is but an artifice, a sop to vanity,
is but a flower by the breezes bowed,
is but a ploy to counter destiny,
    is but a foolish labor, ill-employed,
is but a fancy, and, as all may see,
is but cadaver, ashes, shadow, void.

Quéjase de la suerte: insinúa su aversión a los vicios, y justifica su divertimiento a las Musas

En perseguirme, Mundo ¿qué interesas?
¿En qué te ofendo, cuando sólo intento
poner bellezas en mi entendimiento
y no mi entendimiento en las bellezas?
    Yo no estimo tesoros ni riquezas;
y así, siempre me causa más contento
poner riquezas en mi pensamiento
que no mi pensamiento en las riquezas.
    Y no estimo hermosura que, vencida,
es despojo civil de las edades,
ni riqueza me agrada fementida,
    teniendo por mejor, en mis verdades,
consumir vanidades de la vida
que consumir la vida en vanidades.

*She Laments Her Fortune, She Hints
of Her Aversion to All Vice, and Justifies
Her Diversion with the Muses*

    In my pursuit, World, why such diligence?
What my offense, when I am thus inclined,
insuring elegance affect my mind,
not that my mind affect an elegance?
    I have no love of riches or finánce,
and thus do I most happily, I find,
expend finances to enrich my mind
and not my mind expend upon finánce.
    I worship beauty not, but vilify
that spoil of time that mocks eternity,
nor less, deceitful treasures glorify,
    but hold as foremost in my hierarchy
consuming all the vanity in life,
and not consuming life in vanity.

148

Escoge antes el morir que exponerse a los ultrajes de la vejez

Miró Celia una rosa que en el prado
ostentaba feliz la pompa vana
y con afeites de carmín y grana
bañaba alegre el rostro delicado;
   y dijo:—Goza, sin temor del Hado,
el curso breve de tu edad lozana,
pues no podrá la muerte de mañana
quitarte lo que hubieres hoy gozado;
   y aunque llega la muerte presurosa
y tu fragante vida se te aleja,
no sientas el morir tan bella y moza:
   mira que la experiencia te aconseja
que es fortuna morirte siendo hermosa
y no ver el ultraje de ser vieja.

Better Death Than Suffer the Affronts
of Growing Old

    In the gardens, Celia gazed upon a rose
that candid in its haughty ostentation,
and bright in tints of scarlet and rich crimson,
joyfully its fragile face exposed,
    and said: "Enjoy the day, fear not the blows
of Fate in this too fleeting celebration,
the death that on the morrow claims its portion,
cannot take from you the joys this day bestows;
    though the perfume of life fade on the air,
and the hour of your passing too soon toll,
fear not the death that finds you young and fair:
    take the counsel that experience extols,
to die while beautiful is finer far
than to suffer the affront of growing old."

Encarece de animosidad la elección
de estado durable hasta la muerte

Si los riesgos del mar considerara,
ninguno se embarcara; si antes viera
bien su peligro, nadie se atreviera
ni al bravo toro osado provocara.
Si del fogoso bruto ponderara
la furia desbocada en la carrera
el jinete prudente, nunca hubiera
quien con discreta mano lo enfrenara.
Pero si hubiera alguno tan osado
que, no obstante el peligro, al mismo Apolo
quisiese gobernar con atrevida
mano el rápido carro en luz bañado,
todo lo hiciera, y no tomara sólo
estado que ha de ser toda la vida.

Spiritedly, She Considers the Choice of a State Enduring Unto Death

Were the perils of the ocean fully weighed,
no man would voyage, or, could he but read
the hidden dangers, knowingly proceed
or dare to bait the bull to frenzied rage.

Were prudent rider overly dismayed,
should he contemplate the fury of his steed
or ponder where its headlong course might lead,
there'd be no reining hand to be obeyed.

But were there one so daring, one so bold
that, heedless of the danger, he might place,
upon Apollo's reins, emboldened hand

to guide the fleeting chariot bathed in gold,
the diversity of life he would embrace
and never choose a state to last his span.

Sospecha crueldad disimulada, el alivio que la Esperanza da

Diuturna enfermedad de la Esperanza,
que así entretienes mis cansados años
y en el fiel de los bienes y los daños
tienes en equilibrio la balanza;
        que siempre suspendida, en la tardanza
de inclinarse, no dejan tus engaños
que lleguen a excederse en los tamaños
la desesperación o confianza:
        ¿quién te ha quitado el nombre de homicida?
Pues lo eres más severa, si se advierte
que suspendes el alma entretenida;
        y entre la infausta o la felice suerte,
no lo haces tu por conservar la vida
sino por dar más dilatada muerte.

She Distrusts, as Disguised Cruelty, the Solace Offered by Hope

Oh, malady of Hope, your persistence
sustains the passing of my weary years,
while measuring my wishes and my fears
your balances maintain equivalence;
deceitfully, and with what indolence,
the pans begin to tip, but as change nears
invariably your parity adheres:
despair is counterpoised by confidence.
Still, Murderess is how you must be known,
for Murderess you are, when it is owned
between a fate of happiness or strife
my soul has hung suspended far too long;
you do not act thus to prolong my life
but, rather, that in life death be prolonged.

161 (III)

Inés, yo con tu amor me *refocilo*,
y viéndome querer me *regodeo*;
en mirar tu hermosura me *recreo*,
y cuando estás celosa me *reguilo*.

Si a otro miras, de celos me *aniquilo*,
y tiemblo de tu gracia y tu *meneo*;
porque sé, Inés, que tú con un *voleo*
no dejarás humor ni aun para *quilo*.

Cuando estás enojada no *resuello*,
cuando me das picones me *refino*,
cuando sales de casa no *reposo*;

y espero, Inés, que entre esto y entre *aquello*,
tu amor, acompañado de mi *vino*,
dé conmigo en la cama o en el *coso*.

161 (III)*

Inés, dear, with your love I am *enraptured*,
and as object of your love, I am *enthralled*,
when gazing on your beauty I am *captured*,
but when I find you jealous, want to *bawl*.

I die of jealousy if others you *entangle*,
I tremble at your grace, your step *sublime*,
because I know, Inés, that you could *mangle*,
the humors of my systematic *chyme*.

When I hold your dainty hand, I am *aquiver*,
in your anger, feel that I must soon *expire*,
if you venture from your home I am *adither*,

so I say, Inés, to one thing I *aspire*,
that your love and my good wine will draw you *hither*,
and to tumble you to bed I can *conspire*.

* One of Five Burlesque Sonnets in Which the Poet-
ess Was Circumscribed by Rhymes Which Had
Been Determined; Composed in a Moment of
Relaxation

En que satisface un recelo con la retórica del llanto

Esta tarde, mi bien, cuando te hablaba,
como en tu rostro y tus acciones veía
que con palabras no te persuadía,
que el corazón me vieses deseaba;

y Amor, que mis intentos ayudaba,
venció lo que imposible parecía:
pues entre el llanto, que el dolor vertía,
el corazón deshecho destilaba.

Baste ya de rigores, mi bien, baste;
no te atormenten más celos tiranos,
ni el vil recelo tu quietud contraste

con sombras necias, con indicios vanos,
pues ya en líquido humor viste y tocaste
mi corazón deshecho entre tus manos.

She Answers Suspicions In the Rhetoric of Tears

My love, this evening when I spoke with you,
and in your face and actions I could read
that arguments of words you would not heed,
my heart I longed to open to your view.

In this intention, Love my wishes knew
and, though they seemed impossible, achieved:
pouring in tears that sorrow had conceived,
with every beat my heart dissolved anew.

Enough of suffering, my love, enough:
let jealousy's vile tyranny be banned,
let no suspicious thought your calm corrupt

with foolish gloom by futile doubt enhanced,
for now, this afternoon, you saw and touched
my heart, dissolved and liquid in your hands.

Que contiene una fantasía contenta con amor decente

Detente, sombra de mi bien esquivo,
imagen del hechizo que más quiero,
bella ilusión por quien alegre muero,
dulce ficción por quien penosa vivo.

Si al imán de tus gracias, atractivo,
sirve mi pecho de obediente acero,
¿para qué me enamoras lisonjero
si has de burlarme luego fugitivo?

Mas blasonar no puedes, satisfecho,
de que triunfa de mí tu tiranía:
que aunque dejas burlado el lazo estrecho

que tu forma fantástica ceñía,
poco importa burlar brazos y pecho
si te labra prisión mi fantasía.

Which Recounts How Fantasy Contents Itself with Honorable Love

Stay, shadow of contentment too short-lived,
illusion of enchantment I most prize,
fair image for whom happily I die,
sweet fiction for whom painfully I live.

If answering your charms' imperative,
compliant, I like steel to magnet fly,
by what logic do you flatter and entice,
only to flee, a taunting fugitive?

'Tis no triumph that you so smugly boast
that I fell victim to your tyranny;
though from encircling bonds that held you fast

your elusive form too readily slipped free,
and though to my arms you are forever lost,
you are a prisoner in my fantasy.

166

Resuelve la cuestión de cuál sea pesar
más molesto en encontradas correspondencias,
amar o aborrecer.

Que no me quiera Fabio, al verse amado,
es dolor sin igual en mí sentido;
mas que me quiera Silvio, aborrecido,
es menor mal, mas no menos enfado.
    ¿Qué sufrimiento no estará cansado
si siempre le resuenan al oído
tras la vana arrogancia de un querido
el cansado gemir de un desdeñado?
    Si de Silvio me cansa el rendimiento,
a Fabio canso con estar rendida;
si de éste busco el agradecimiento,
    a mí me busca el otro agradecida:
por activa y pasiva es mi tormento,
pues padezco en querer y en ser querida.

She Resolves the Question of Which be the More Trying Role in Conflicting Relationships: To Love or to Abhor

That Fabio does not love me, though adored,
is grief unmatched by any I have known,
a lesser hurt, though no less bothersome,
is that Silvio loves me, he in turn abhorred.

What patience, sorely tried, would not deplore,
what ringing ear, assaulted, not bemoan,
the ever-plaintive sighs of one disowned,
the arrogance of a vain conqueror.

If I am bored by Silvio's submission,
it bores Fabio to tears that I submit;
if from Fabio I eternally court permission,

Silvio seeks from me what I permit;
if dual torment is to be my one condition,
both of loving and being loved I would be quit.

Silvas

Hepta- and hendecasyllabic lines alternating
without one set pattern, and with cross rhyme

Fragmento del Primero sueño

Piramidal, funesta, de la tierra
nacida sombra, al Cielo encaminaba
de vanos obeliscos punta altiva,
escalar pretendiendo las Estrellas;
si bien sus luces bellas
—exentas siempre, siempre rutilantes—
la tenebrosa guerra
que con negros vapores le intimaba
la pavorosa sombra fugitiva
burlaban tan distantes,
que su atezado ceño
al superior convexo aun no llegaba
del orbe de la Diosa
que tres veces hermosa
con tres hermosos rostros ser ostenta,
quedando sólo dueño
del aire que empañaba
con el aliento denso que exhalaba;
y en la quietud contenta
de imperio silencioso,
sumisas sólo voces consentía
de las nocturnas aves,
tan obscuras, tan graves
que aun el silencio no se interrumpía.
    Con tardo vuelo y canto, del oído
mal, y aun peor del ánimo admitido,
la avergonzada Nictimene acecha
de las sagradas puertas los resquicios,
o de las claraboyas eminentes
los huecos más propicios
que capaz a su intento le abren brecha,

Fragment from First Dream

Pyramidal, doleful, mournful shadow
born of the earth, the haughty culmination
of vain obelisks thrust toward the Heavens,
attempting to ascend and touch the Stars
whose resplendent glow
(unobscured, eternal scintillation)
mocked from afar
the tenebrous war
blackly intimated in the vapors
of the awesome, fleeting adumbration;
this glowering cloud
that reached the rim did not in all absorb
the Goddess's orb
(three, Diana's faces
that show her beauteous being in three phases),
but conquered only air,
misted the atmosphere
that darkened densely with each exhalation;
and in the quietude
of this silent kingdom
only muted voices could be heard
from nocturnal birds,
so solemn and subdued
the muffled sound did not disturb the silence.
    In flight and song ungraceful, dull of ear,
and poorer still in quality of soul,
humiliated, poor Nictímene
lurks hidden at the chinks in sacred doors,
hovers at a high clerestory,
seeks the propitious rift,
that will intrigue to open to her scheme,

y sacrílega llega a los lucientes
faroles sacros de perenne llama
que extingue, si no infama,
en licor claro la materia crasa
consumiendo, que el árbol de Minerva
de su fruto, de prensas agravado,
congojoso sudó y rindió forzado.
    Y aquellas que su casa
campo vieron volver, sus telas hierba,
a la deidad de Baco inobedientes
—ya no historias contando diferentes,
en forma sí afrentosa transformadas—,
segunda forman niebla,
ser vistas aun temiendo en la tiniebla,
aves sin pluma aladas:
aquellas tres oficïosas, digo,
atrevidas Hermanas,
que el tremendo castigo
de desnudas les dio pardas membranas
alas tan mal dispuestas
que escarnio son aun de las más funestas:
éstas, con el parlero
ministro de Plutón un tiempo, ahora
supersticioso indicio al agorero,
solos la no canora
componían capilla pavorosa,
máximas, negras, longas entonando,
y pausas más que voces, esperando
a la torpe mensura perezosa
de mayor proporción tal vez, que el viento
con flemático echaba movimiento,
de tan tardo compás, tan detenido,
que en medio se quedó tal vez dormido.
    Este, pues, triste són intercadente
de la asombrada turba temerosa,

and sacrilegiously draws near the gleam
of holy lamps where burn eternal flames
that she extinguishes,
if not defames, imbibing as a clear
liquor the heavy oil unwilling
relinquished, its fruit oppressed by presses,
the tortured sweat wrung from Minerva's tree.
      And those women, three,
their home become a field, their weaving, weeds,
for want of faith in Bacchus's deity
(no longer telling of heroic deeds,
but by dishonor hideously transformed)
now form a second fog,
fearful, even by dark, to be perceived,
winged, naked birds;
these three of whom I speak, diligent,
audacious Sisters,
as dreadful punishment
with dark membraneous pinions were aggrieved,
wings monstrously conceived,
a mockery, but also piteous;
they, and that Ascálaphus,
once Pluto's loose-tongued minister, but now
a sign most sinister to augerers,
among them formed
a tuneless and appaling a capella,
black maximas and longas they intoned,
their singing, though, more silences than sound,
hoping, perhaps, the apathetic drone
might quicken in intensity, or else,
phlegmatically, the wind might stir to song,
a tempo so lethargically composed
that in its midst, the very wind might doze.
      This gloomy, then, and fluctuating strain,
from the adumbral, awe-inspiring throng,

menos a la atención solicitaba
que al sueño persuadía;
antes sí, lentamente,
su obtusa consonancia espacïosa
al sosiego inducía
y al reposo los miembros convidaba
—el silencio intimando a los vivientes,
uno y otro sellando labio obscuro
con indicante dedo,
Harpócrates, la noche, silencioso;
a cuyo, aunque no duro,
si bien imperioso
precepto, todos fueron obedientes—.
　　El viento sosegado, el can dormido,
éste yace, aquél quedo
los átomos no mueve,
con el susurro hacer temiendo leve,
aunque poco, sacrílego rüido,
violador del silencio sosegado.
El mar, no ya alterado,
ni aun la instable mecía
cerúlea cuna donde el Sol dormía;
y los dormidos, siempre mudos, peces,
en los lechos lamosos
de sus obscuros senos cavernosos,
mudos eran dos veces;
y entre ellos, la engañosa encantadora
Alcione, a los que antes
en peces transformó, simples amantes,
transformada también, vengaba ahora.
　　En los del monte senos escondidos,
cóncavos de peñascos mal formados
—de su aspereza menos defendidos
que de su obscuridad asegurados—,
cuya mansión sombría
ser puede noche en la mitad del día,

less than a summoning to wakefulness,
persuasion was to dream,
but gradually, it seems;
first, the prolonged and consonant refrain
invited peacefulness,
lulling the body gently to its rest
—and there, sealing all lips, imposing quiet,
his will conveyed to every living thing,
his finger cautioning,
Harpócrates, the god of silence, night;
and to what if not
unjust, might well be thought
imperious command, all did attend.
    The breeze becalmed, the tranquil dog adoze,
both at rest, such is the mood
the still air not an atom moves
for fear its faintest murmur might disclose
an innocent but sacrilegious hum,
a profanation of the soothing calm.
A settled, stable sea,
the cerulean cradle
of the deep unrocked, the sun asleep;
the fish forever dumb, and somnolent,
idle in dark ooze
within a caverned, murky firmament,
were twice, were doubly mute;
and found among them was Alcýone,
the artful sorceress
who having changed her suitors into fish
was herself transmuted in redress.
    In the hidden bosom of the mountain,
uneven domes of concave, rugged stone
(far less against adversity insured
than of continuing obscurity assured),
in this somber mansion
where night may fall while day is at the noon,

incógnita aún al cierto
montaraz pie del cazador experto
—despuesta la fiereza
de unos, y de otros el temor depuesto—
yacía el vulgo bruto,
a la Naturaleza
el de su potestad pagando impuesto,
universal tributo;
y el Rey, que vigilancias afectaba,
aun con abiertos ojos no velaba. . . .

a landscape still unknown
to even skilled and practiced forest huntsmen
(the huntsmen without fear,
the hunters from ferocity released)
lay a noble beast,
and in obeïsance,
the brute to Nature's worldly sovereignty
consigned the just tribute;
and though this King affected vigilance,
sleeping with open eyes, it did not see. . . .

Villancicos

Religious songs in various forms

This little Nahuatl ballad on the Assumption of the Virgin is one of two *tocotines*, or Indian-style dance songs, composed by Sor Juana Inés de la Cruz. (The other is in mixed Nahuatl and Spanish.) As published by Sor Juana, the piece forms part of a larger *ensaladilla*, or satire, purporting to show how Blacks and Indians might react to the Virgin's rise to heaven. After a farcical dialogue in pidgin Spanish between two *negrillos*, the Indians appear, singing sweetly (*con voces suaves*) in untranslated Nahuatl. Owing to the misspellings, the odd grammar, and Sor Juana's tendency to fill out her trimeter with extra syllables, the words are difficult to recognize. Although the late Angel M. Garibay provided a Spanish gloss, the following is believed to be the first attempt at a connected translation.

John Bierhorst

Tla ya timohuica,
totlazo Zuapilli,
maca ammo, Tonantzin,
titechmoilcahuíliz.
　Ma nel in Ilhuícac
huel timomaquítiz,
¿amo nozo quenman
timotlalnamíctiz?
　In moayolque mochtin
huel motilinizque;
tlaca amo, tehuatzin
ticmomatlaníliz
　Ca mitztlacamati
motlazo Piltzintli,
mac tel, in tepampa
xicmotlatlauhtili.
　Tlaca ammo quinequi,
xicmoilnamiquili
ca monacayotzin
oticmomaquiti.
　Mochichihualayo
oquimomitili,
tla motemictía
ihuan Tetepitzin.
　Ma mopampantzinco
in moayolcatintin,
in itla pohpoltin,
tictomacehuizque.
　Totlatlácol mochtin
tïololquiztizque;
Ilhuícac tïazque,
timitzittalizque:
　　in campa cemícac
timonemitíliz,
cemícac mochíhuaz
in monahuatiltzin.

Sor Juana Inés de la Cruz,
1676

Please don't go,
dear lady.
Don't leave us,
dear mother.
    Will you
remember us,
if you go
to heaven?
    All your people
will suffer. Please
don't be the one
to hurt them.
    Your dear son
obeys you.
Pray to him
for us.
    Let him not
want. Remember
how you fed him
from your body:
    he drank
your milk.
And let him dream,
the little one.
    As for us,
your people,
allow us to be
worthy of something:
    all of us will
rid our hearts
of sin and come see
you in heaven,
    where you
live forever,
where you
rule forever.

John Bierhorst

    Blessed lady,
do not go.
Mother, do not
cause us woe.
    If to heaven
you ascend,
will you still
your love extend?
    All your people
will lament.
Do not add to
their torment.
    Your dear son
will heed your word.
Let your prayer
for us be heard.
    Now let him from
want be free;
for once he fed
from your body:
    he drank your milk,
the little one,
now to dreams
let him succumb.
    We are your people,
as for us,
may we be worthy
and righteous:
    all our hearts
we'll rid of sin,
and come to see you
in Heaven,
    where you will
live on forever,
where you are
enthroned forever.

Margaret Sayers Peden

317 *Villancico VI*

¡Víctor, víctor Catarina,
que con su ciencia divina
los sabios ha convencido,
y victoriosa ha salido
—con su ciencia soberana—
de la arrogancia profana
que a convencerla ha venido!
¡Víctor, víctor, víctor!

COPLAS

De una Mujer se convencen
todos los Sabios de Egipto,
para prueba de que el sexo
no es escencia en lo entendido.
¡Víctor, víctor!
     Prodigio fue, y aun milagro;
pero no estuvo el prodigio
en vencerlos, sino en que
ellos se den por vencidos.
¡Víctor, víctor!
     ¡Qué bien se ve que eran Sabios
en confesarse rendidos,
que es triunfo el obedecer
de la razón el dominio!
¡Víctor, víctor!
     Las luces de la verdad
no se obscurecen con gritos;
que su eco sabe valiente
sobresalir del rüido.
¡Víctor, víctor!
     No se avergüenzan los Sabios
de mirarse convencidos;
porque saben, como Sabios,
que su saber es finito.
¡Víctor, víctor!

317 *Villancico VI, from SANTA CATARINA, 1691*

Victor! Victor! Catherine,
who with enlightenment divine
persuaded all the learned men,
she who with triumph overcame
—with knowledge truly sovereign—
the pride and arrogance profane
of those who challenged her, in vain
Victor! Victor! Victor!

VERSES

There in Egypt, all the sages
by a woman were convinced
that gender is not of the essence
in matters of intelligence.
Victor! Victor!

    A victory, a miracle;
though more prodigious than the feat
of conquering, was surely that
the men themselves declared defeat.
Victor! Victor!

    How wise they were, these Prudent Men,
acknowledging they were outdone,
for one conquers when one yields
to wisdom greater than one's own.
Victor! Victor!

    Illumination shed by truth
will never by mere shouts be drowned;
persistently, its echo rings,
above all obstacles resounds.
Victor! Victor!

    None of these Wise Men was ashamed
when he found himself convinced,
because, in being Wise, he knew
his knowledge was not infinite.
Victor! Victor!

Estudia, arguye y enseña,
y es de la Iglesia servicio,
que no la quiere ignorante
El que racional la hizo.
¡Víctor, víctor!

    ¡Oh, qué soberbios vendrían,
al juntarlos Maximino!
Mas salieron admirados
los que entraron presumidos.
¡Víctor, víctor!

    Vencidos, con ella todos
la vida dan al cuchillo:
¡oh cuánto bien se perdiera
si Docta no hubiera sido!
¡Víctor, víctor!

    Nunca de varón ilustre
triunfo igual habemos visto;
y es que quiso Dios en ella
honrar el sexo femíneo.
¡Víctor, víctor!

    Ocho y diez vueltas del Sol,
era el espacio florido
de su edad; mas de su ciencia
¿quién podrá contar los siglos?
¡Víctor, víctor!

    Perdióse (¡oh dolor!) la forma
de sus doctos silogismos:
pero, los que no con tinta,
dejó con su sangre escritos.
¡Víctor, víctor!

    Tutelar sacra Patrona,
es de las Letras Asilo;
porque siempre ilustre Sabios,
quien Santos de Sabios hizo.
¡Víctor, víctor!

It is of service to the Church
that women argue, tutor, learn,
for He Who granted women reason
would not have them uninformed.
Victor! Victor!

How haughtily they must have come,
the men that Maximin convened,
though at their advent arrogant,
they left with wonder and esteem.
Victor! Victor!

Persuaded, all of them, with her,
gave up their lives unto the knife:
how much good might have been lost,
were Catherine less erudite!
Victor! Victor!

No man, whatever his renown,
accomplished such a victory,
and we know that God, through her,
honored femininity.
Victor! Victor!

Too brief, the flowering of her years,
but ten and eight, the sun's rotations,
but when measuring her knowledge,
who could sum the countless ages?
Victor! Victor!

Now all her learned arguments
are lost to us (how great the grief).
But with her blood, if not with ink,
she wrote the lesson of her life.
Victor! Victor!

Tutelar and holy Patron,
Catherine, the Shrine of Arts;
long may she illumine Wise Men,
she who Wise to Saints converts.
Victor! Victor!

Theater, Sacred
and Profane

Loa para el Auto sacramental de "El divino Narciso"

por alegorías

Personas que hablan en ella

El Occidente	La Religión
La América	Músicos
El Celo	Soldados

Loa for the Auto sacramental
"The Divine Narcissus"

through allegories

Cast of Characters

Occident	Religion
America	Musicians
Zeal	Soldiers

Escena I

Sale el OCCIDENTE, Indio galán, con corona, y la AMÉRI-
CA, a su lado, de India bizarra: con mantas y huipiles, al
modo que se canta el Tocotín. Siéntanse en dos sillas; y
por una parte y otra bailan Indios e Indias, con plumas y
sonajas en las manos, como se hace de ordinario esta
Danza; y mientras bailan, canta la Música.

MÚSICA

Nobles Mejicanos,
cuya estirpe antigua,
de las claras luces
del Sol se origina:
Pues hoy es del año
el dichoso día
en que se consagra
la mayor Reliquia,
¡venid adornados
de vuestras divisas,
y a la devoción
se una la alegría:
y en pompa festiva,
celebrad al gran Dios de las Semillas!

MÚSICA

Y pues la abundancia
de nuestras provincias
se Le debe al que es
Quien las fertiliza,
ofreced devotos,
pues Le son debidas,
de los nuevos frutos
todas las primicias.
¡Dad de vuestras venas
la sangre más fina,
para que, mezclada,
a su culto sirva;

Scene I

Enter OCCIDENT, a stately Indian wearing a crown, and
AMERICA beside him, a noble Indian woman, in the *man-tas* and *huipiles* worn when singing a *tocotín*. They sit in
two chairs; several Indian men and women dance holding
feathers and rattles in their hands, as is traditional during
this celebration; as they dance, MUSIC sings:

MUSIC

> Most noble Mexicans,
> whose ancient origin
> is found in the brilliant rays
> cast like arrows by the Sun,
> mark well the time of year,
> this day is given to laud
> and honor in our way
> the highest of our gods.
> Come clad in ornaments
> of your station the sign,
> and to your piety
> let happiness be joined:
> with festive pageantry
> worship the all-powerful God of Seeds!

MUSIC

> The riches of our lands
> in copious plenteousness
> are owing to the one
> who makes them bounteous.
> So bring your fervent thanks,
> and at the harvest time,
> give unto Him his due,
> the first fruit of the vine.
> Let flow the purest blood,
> give from your own veins,
> to blend with many bloods
> and thus His cult sustain.

y en pompa festiva,
celebrad al gran Dios de las Semillas!

(*Siéntanse el* OCCIDENTE *y la* AMÉRICA, *y cesa la música.*)

OCCIDENTE

Pues entre todos los Dioses
que mi culto solemniza,
aunque son tantos, que sólo
en aquesta esclarecida
Ciudad Regia, de dos mil
pasan, a quien sacrifica
en sacrificios crüentos
de humana sangre vertida,
ya las entrañas que pulsan,
ya el corazón que palpita;
aunque son (vuelvo a decir)
tantos, entre todos mira
mi atención, como a mayor,
al gran Dios de las Semillas.

AMÉRICA

Y con razón, pues es solo
el que nuestra Monarquía
sustenta, pues la abundancia
de los frutos se Le aplica;
y como éste es el mayor
beneficio, en quien se cifran
todos los otros, pues lo es
el de conservar la vida,
como el mayor Lo estimamos:
pues ¿qué importara que rica
el América abundara
en el oro de sus minas,
si esterilizando el campo
sus fumosidades mismas,
no dejaran a los frutos
que en sementeras opimas
brotasen? Demás de que

With festive pageantry
worship the all-powerful God of Seeds!

(OCCIDENT *and* AMERICA *sit, as* MUSIC *ceases.*)

OCCIDENT

So great in number are the Gods
that our religion sanctifies,
so many in this place alone
the many rites we solemnize,
that this our Royal City is
the scene of cruelest sacrifice:
two thousand gods are satisfied,
but human blood must be the price;
now see the entrails that still throb,
now see hearts that redly beat,
and though the gods are myriad,
our gods so many (I repeat),
the greatest God among them all
is our Great God, the God of Seeds!

AMERICA

And rightly so, for He alone
has long sustained our monarchy,
for all the riches of the field
we owe to Him our fealty,
and as the greatest benefice,
in which all others are contained,
is that abundance of the land,
our life and breath by it maintained,
we name Him greatest of the Gods.
What matters all the glittering gold
in which America abounds,
what value precious ores untold,
if their excrescences befoul
and sterilize a fertile earth,
if no fruits ripen, no maize grows,
and no tender buds spring forth?
But the protection of this God

su protección no limita
sólo a corporal sustento
de la material comida,
sino que después, haciendo
manjar de sus carnes mismas
(estando purificadas
antes, de sus inmundicias
corporales), de las manchas
el Alma nos purifica.
Y así, atentos a su culto,
todos conmigo repitan:

ELLOS, y MÚSICA

¡En pompa festiva,
celebrad al gran Dios de las Semillas!

Escena II

(*Éntranse bailando; y salen la* RELIGIÓN CRISTIANA, *de
Dama Española, y el* CELO, *de Capitán General, armado;
y detrás,* SOLDADOS *Españoles.*)

RELIGIÓN

¿Cómo, siendo el Celo tú,
sufren tus cristianas iras
ver que, vanamente ciega,
celebre la Idolatría
con supersticiosos cultos
un Ídolo, en ignominia
de la Religión Cristiana?

CELO

Religión: no tan aprisa
de mi omisión te querelles,
te quejes de mis caricias;
pues ya levantado el brazo,

is broader than continuance,
with the provision of our food,
of our daily sustenance,
He makes a paste of His own flesh,
and we partake with veneration
(though first the paste is purified
of bodily contamination),
and so our Soul he purifies
of all its blemishes and stains.
And thus in homage to His cult,
may everyone with me proclaim:

ALL *and* MUSIC

In festive pageantry,
worship the all-powerful God of Seeds!

Scene II

(*They exit, dancing, and then enter* CHRISTIAN RELIGION,
as a Spanish Lady, and ZEAL, *as a Captain General,
armed; behind them, Spanish* SOLDIERS.

RELIGION

How is it, then, as you are Zeal,
your Christian wrath can tolerate
that here with blind conformity
they bow before Idolatry,
and, superstitious, elevate
an Idol, with effrontery,
above our Christianity?

ZEAL

Religion, do not be dismayed:
my compassion you upbraid,
my tolerance you disavow,
but see, I stand before you now

ya blandida la cuchilla
traigo, para tus venganzas.
Tú a ese lado te retiras
mientras vengo tus agravios.

(*Salen, bailando, el* OCCIDENTE *y* AMÉRICA, *y Acompaña-
miento y Música, por otro lado*)

MÚSICA

¡Y en pompa festiva,
celebrad al gran Dios de las Semillas!

CELO

Pues ya ellos salen, yo llego.

RELIGIÓN

Yo iré también, que me inclina
la piedad a llegar (antes
que tu furor los embista)
a convidarlos, de paz,
a que mi culto reciban.

CELO

Pues lleguemos, que en sus torpes
ritos está entretenida.

MÚSICA

¡Y en pompa festiva,
celebrad al gran Dios de las Semillas!

(*Llegan el* CELO *y la* RELIGIÓN)

RELIGIÓN

Occidente poderoso,
América bella y rica,
que vivís tan miserables
entre las riquezas mismas:
dejad el culto profano
a que el Demonio os incita.
¡Abrid los ojos! Seguid

with arm upraised, unsheathed my blade,
which I address to your revenge.
And now, retire, your cares allayed,
as their transgressions I avenge.

(*Enter, dancing,* OCCIDENT *and* AMERICA, *and from the
other side,* MUSIC, *with accompaniment*)

MUSIC

And with festive pageantry,
worship the all-powerful God of Seeds!

ZEAL

They are here. I will approach.

RELIGION

And I as well, with all compassion,
for I would go with tones of peace
(before unleashing your aggression)
to urge them to accept my word,
and in the faith be sanctified.

ZEAL

Then let us go, for even now
they practice their revolting rite.

MUSIC

And with festive pageantry,
worship the great God of Seeds!

(ZEAL *and* RELIGION *approach*)

RELIGION

Hear me, mighty Occident,
America, so beautiful,
your lives are led in misery
though your land is bountiful.
Abandon this unholy cult
which the Devil doth incite.
Open your eyes. Accept my word

la verdadera Doctrina
que mi amor os persüade.

OCCIDENTE

¿Qué gentes no conocidas
son éstas que miro, ¡Cielos!,
que así de mis alegrías
quieren impedir el curso?

AMÉRICA

¿Qué Naciones nunca vistas
quieren oponerse al fuero
de mi potestad antigua?

OCCIDENTE

¡Oh tú, extranjera Belleza;
¡oh tú, Mujer peregrina!
Dime quién eres, que vienes
a perturbar mis delicias.

RELIGIÓN

Soy la Religión Cristiana,
que intento que tus Provincias
se reduzcan a mi culto.

OCCIDENTE

¡Buen empeño solicitas!

AMÉRICA

¡Buena locura pretendes!

OCCIDENTE

¡Buen imposible maquinas!

AMÉRICA

Sin duda es loca; ¡dejadla,
y nuestros cultos prosigan!

and follow in the Path of Light,
fully persuaded by my love.

OCCIDENT

These unknown persons, who are they
who now before my presence stand?
Oh gods, who ventures thus to stay
the festive moment's rightful course?

AMERICA

What Nations these, which none has seen?
Do they come here to interfere,
my ancient power contravene?

OCCIDENT

Oh, Lovely Beauty, who are you,
fair Pilgrim from another nation?
I ask you now, why have you come
to interrupt my celebration?

RELIGION

Christian Religion is my name,
and I propose that all will bend
before the power of my word.

OCCIDENT

A great endeavor you intend!

AMERICA

A great madness you display!

OCCIDENT

The inconceivable you scheme!

AMERICA

She must be mad, ignore her now,
let them continue with our theme!

MÚSICA y ELLOS

¡Y en pompa festiva,
celebrad al gran Dios de las Semillas!

CELO

¿Cómo, bárbara Occidente:
¿cómo, ciega Idolatría,
a la Religión desprecias,
mi dulce Esposa querida?
Pues mira que a tus maldades
ya has llenado la medida,
y que no permite Dios
que en tus delitos prosigas,
y me envía a castigarte.

OCCIDENTE

¿Quién eres, que atemorizas
con sólo ver tu semblante?

CELO

El Celo soy. ¿Qué te admira?
Que, cuando a la Religión
desprecian tus demasías,
entrará el Celo a vengarla
castigando tu osadía.
Ministro de Dios soy, que
viendo que tus tiranías
han llegado ya a lo sumo,
cansado de ver que vivas
tantos años entre errores,
a castigarte me envía.
Y así, estas armadas Huestes,
que rayos de acero vibran,
ministros son de Su enojo
e instrumentos de Sus iras.

OCCIDENTE

¿Qué Dios, qué error, qué torpeza,
o qué castigos me intimas?

ALL *and* MUSIC

With festive pageantry,
worship the all-powerful God of Seeds!

ZEAL

How, barbaric Occident,
and you, oh blind Idolatry,
can you presume to scorn my Wife,
beloved Christianity?
For brimming to the vessel's lip
we see your sinful degradation;
the Lord our God will not allow
That you continue in transgression,
and He sends me to punish you.

OCCIDENT

And who are you, who terrorize
all those who gaze upon your face?

ZEAL

I am Zeal. Whence your surprise?
For when Religion you would scorn
with practices of vile excess,
then Zeal must enter on the scene
to castigate your wickedness.
I am a Minister from God
Who, witnessing your tyranny,
the error of these many years
of lives lived in barbarity,
has reached the limits of His grace
and sends His punishment through me.
And thus these armed and mighty Hosts
whose gleaming blades of steel you see
are His ministers of wrath,
the instruments of Holy rage.

OCCIDENT

What god, what error, what offense,
what punishment do you presage?

Que no entiendo tus razones
ni aun por remotas noticias,
ni quién eres tú, que osado
a tanto empeño te animas
como impedir que mi gente
en debidos cultos diga:

MÚSICA

¡Y en pompa festiva,
celebrad al gran Dios de las Semillas!

AMÉRICA

Bárbaro, loco, que ciego,
con razones no entendidas,
quieres turbar el sosiego
que en serena paz tranquila
gozamos: ¡cesa en tu intento,
si no quieres que, en cenizas
reducido, ni aun los vientos
tengan de tu sér noticias!
Y tú, Esposo, y tus vasallos,

(*Al Occidente*)

negad el oído y vista
a sus razones, no haciendo
caso de sus fantasías:
y proseguid vuestros cultos,
sin dejar que advenedizas
Naciones, osadas quieran
intentar interrumpirlas.

MÚSICA

¡Y en pompa festiva,
celebrad al gran Dios de las Semillas!

CELO

Pues la primera propuesta
de paz desprecias altiva,
la segunda, de la guerra,

I do not understand your words,
nor does your argument persuade;
I know you not, who, brazenly,
would thus our rituals invade
and with such zeal that you prevent
that in just worship people say:

MUSIC

With festive pageantry,
worship the great God of Seeds!

AMERICA

Oh, mad, blind, barbaric man,
disturbing our serenity,
you bring confusing arguments
to counter our tranquillity;
you must immediately cease,
unless it is your wish to find
all here assembled turned to ash
with no trace even on the wind!
And you, Husband, and your vassals,

(to OCCIDENT)

you must close your ears and eyes,
do not heed their fantasies,
do not listen to their lies;
proceed, continue with your rites!
Our rituals shall not be banned
by these Nations, still unknown,
so newly come unto our land.

MUSIC

And with festive pageantry,
worship the great God of Seeds!

ZEAL

As our first offering of peace
you have so haughtily disdained,
accept the second, that of war,

será preciso que admitas.
¡Toca al arma! ¡Guerra, guerra!

(*Suenan cajas y clarines*)

OCCIDENTE

¿Qué abortos el Cielo envía
contra mí? ¿Qué armas son éstas,
nunca de mis ojos vistas?
¡Ah, de mis Guardas! ¡Soldados:
las flechas que prevenidas
están siempre, disparad!

AMÉRICA

¿Qué rayos el Cielo vibra
contra mí? ¿Qué fieros globos
de plomo ardiente graniza?
¿Qué Centauros monstrüosos
contra mis gentes militan?

(*Dentro*:)

¡Arma, arma! ¡Guerra, guerra!

(*Tocan*)

¡Viva España! ¡Su Rey viva!

(*Trabada la batalla, van entrándose por una puerta, y salen por otra huyendo los* INDIOS, *y los* ESPAÑOLES *en su alcance; y detrás, el* OCCIDENTE *retirándose de la* RELIGIÓN, *y* AMÉRICA *del* CELO.)

Escena III

RELIGIÓN

¡Ríndete, altivo Occidente!

OCCIDENTE

Ya es preciso que me rinda
tu valor, no tu razón.

from war we will not be restrained!
War! War! To arms! To arms!

(*Sound of drums and trumpets*)

OCCIDENT

What is this wrath the gods devise?
What are the weapons here displayed
that so confound my awestruck eyes?
Ho, my Soldiers, ho there, Guards!
Those arrows that you hold prepared
now send against the enemy!

AMERICA

Why have the gods their lightning bared
to strike me down? What are these spheres
that fall like fiery leaden hail?
What are these Centaurs, man and horse,
that now my followers assail?

(*Off*)

To arms! To arms! We are at war!

(*Drums and trumpets*)

Long live Spain! Her King we hail!

(*The battle is struck;* INDIANS *enter and flee across the stage, pursued by the* SPANISH; OCCIDENT *and* AMERICA *begin to retreat before* RELIGION *and* ZEAL)

Scene III

RELIGION

Surrender, haughty Occident!

OCCIDENT

Your declarations I defy
and only to your power yield.

CELO

¡Muere, América atrevida!

RELIGIÓN

¡Espera, no le des muerte,
que la necesito viva!

CELO

Pues ¿cómo tú la defiendes,
cuando eres tú la ofendida?

RELIGIÓN

Sí, porque haberla vencido
le tocó a tu valentía,
pero a mi piedad le toca
el conservarle la vida:
porque vencerla por fuerza
te tocó; mas el rendirla
con razón, me toca a mí,
con suavidad persuasiva.

CELO

Si has visto ya la protervia
con que tu culto abominan
ciegos, ¿no es mejor que todos
mueran?

RELIGIÓN

      Cese tu justicia,
Celo; no les des la muerte:
que no quiere mi benigna
condición, que mueran, sino
que se conviertan y vivan.

AMÉRICA

Si el pedir que yo no muera,
y el mostrarte compasiva,
es porque esperas de mí
que me vencerás, altiva

ZEAL

Now bold America must die!

RELIGION

Hold, Zeal, do not strike them dead,
keep America alive!

ZEAL

What, you defend America
when she has your faith reviled?

RELIGION

There is no doubt that her defeat
is owing to your bravery,
but now allowing her to live
is witness to my clemency;
it was your duty, with your force,
to conquer her; but now with reason
I, too, work to vanquish her,
but I shall win with soft persuasion.

ZEAL

But their perversion you have seen,
how they abhor and scorn your Word;
they are blind, is it not better
that they die?

RELIGION

          Put up your sword.
Forebear, Zeal, do not attack,
it is my nature to forgive,
I do not want their immolation,
but conversion, let them live.

AMERICA

If in petitioning for my life,
and in exhibiting compassion,
it is your hope that I will yield,
that you will thus divert my passion,

como antes con corporales,
después con intelectivas
armas, estás engañada;
pues aunque lloro cautiva
mi libertad, ¡mi albedrío
con libertad más crecida
adorará mis Deidades!

OCCIDENTE

Yo ya dije que me obliga
a rendirme a ti la fuerza;
y en esto, claro se explica
que no hay fuerza ni violencia
que a la voluntad impida
sus libres operaciones;
y así, aunque cautivo gima,
¡no me podrás impedir
que acá, en mi corazón, diga
que venero al gran Dios de las Semillas!

Escena IV

RELIGIÓN

Espera, que aquésta no
es fuerza, sino caricia.
¿Qué Dios es ése que adoras?

OCCIDENTE

Es un Dios que fertiliza
los campos que dan los frutos;
a quien los cielos se inclinan,
a Quien la lluvia obedece
y, en fin, es El que nos limpia
los pecados, y después
se hace Manjar, que nos brinda.
¡Mira tú si puede haber,
en la Deidad más benigna,

employing arguments of words
as once before you employed arms,
then you will find yourself deceived,
for though my person come to harm,
and though I weep for liberty,
my liberty of will, will grow,
and I shall still adore my Gods!

OCCIDENT

I have told you, and all know,
that I have bowed before your might,
but this caution you must heed,
that there is no strength or might
that ever can my will impede
from its just course, free of control;
though captive I may moan in pain,
your will can never conquer mine,
and in my heart I will proclaim:
I worship the great God of Seeds!

Scene IV

RELIGION

But wait, for what we offer here
is not might, but gentleness.
What God is this that you adore?

OCCIDENT

The Great Lord of fruitfulness.
He makes fertile all the fields,
all the heavens bow to Him,
it is He the rain obeys,
and finally, of all our sin
He cleanses us, then of His being
makes a feast to nurture us.
Tell me whether there can be,
in a God so bounteous,

más beneficios que haga
ni más que yo te repita!

RELIGIÓN

(*Aparte*)

¡Válgame Dios! ¿Qué dibujos,
qué remedos o qué cifras
de nuestras sacras Verdades
quieren ser estas mentiras?
¡Oh cautelosa Serpiente!
¡Oh Áspid venenoso! ¡Oh Hidra,
que viertes por siete bocas,
de tu ponzoña nociva
toda la mortal cicuta!
¿Hasta dónde tu malicia
quiere remedar de Dios
las sagradas Maravillas?
Pero con tu mismo engaño,
si Dios mi lengua habilita,
te tengo de convencer.

AMÉRICA

¿En qué, suspensa, imaginas?
¿Ves cómo no hay otro Dios
como Aquéste, que confirma
en beneficios Sus obras?

RELIGIÓN

De Pablo con la doctrina
tengo de argüir; pues cuando
a los de Atenas predica
viendo que entre ellos es ley
que muera el que solicita
introducir nuevos Dioses,
como él tiene la noticia
de que a un *Dios no conocido*
ellos un altar dedican,
les dice: "No es Deidad nueva,
sino la no conocida

any greater benefice
than I give in this summary?

RELIGION

(*Aside*)

May God have mercy! What reflection
do I see, what counterfeit,
thus patterned in their evil lies,
to mock our holy sacred Truths?
Oh, wily Serpent, sly Reptile,
oh, venom from the Viper's tooth!
Oh, Hydra, seven-headed beast
whose seven mouths spew, lethally,
rivers of poison on our heads,
how far, and how maliciously,
can you continue in this way
God's sacred Miracles to mime?
Now if God will grace my tongue,
this same deceit I shall refine
and use your arguments to win.

AMERICA

What mischief do you fabricate?
Do you not see there is no God,
none other, who corroborates
in benefices all His works?

RELIGION

Then I shall be like Paul, and speak
from holy doctrine; for when he
had come to preach among the Greeks,
he found in Athens the strict law
that he who sought to introduce
an unfamiliar god, would die,
but as he knew they had the use
of faithful worship in a place
devoted to THE UNKNOWN GOD,
he said: this God I give to you
is not unknown, but One you laud,

que adoráis en este altar,
la que mi voz os publica."
Así yo. . . ¡Occidente, escucha;
oye, ciega Idolatría,
pues en escuchar mis voces
consisten todas tus dichas!

    Esos milagros que cuentas,
esos prodigios que intimas,
esos visos, esos rasgos,
que debajo de cortinas
supersticiosas asoman;
esos portentos que vicias,
atribuyendo su efecto
a tus Deidades mentidas,
obras del Dios Verdadero,
y de Su sabiduría
son efectos. Pues si el prado
florido se fertiliza,
si los campos se fecundan,
si el fruto se multiplica,
si las sementeras crecen,
si las lluvias se destilan,
todo es obra de Su diestra;
pues ni el brazo que cultiva,
ni la lluvia que fecunda,
ni el calor que vivifica,
diera incremento a las plantas
a faltar Su productiva
Providencia, que concurre
a darles vegetativa
alma.

AMÉRICA

    Cuando eso así sea,
díme: ¿Será tan propicia
esa Deidad, que se deje
tocar de mis manos mismas,
como el Ídolo que aquí
mis propias manos fabrican
de semillas y de sangre

you ignorantly worship Him,
now Him declare I unto you.
And thus do I. . . . Hear, Occident,
Idolatry, attend me, too,
for if you listen to my words
you will find salvation there.

      Those many wonders you recount,
the miracles to which you swear,
the shimmering light, the flashing gleam
you glimpsed through Superstition's veil,
the prodigies, the prophecies,
the portents we heard you detail,
attributing their consequence
to your mendacious deities,
are but the work of One True God,
His wisdom and His sovereignty.
For if the flowering meadows bloom
and gardens yield their rich supply,
if the fields are fertilized,
and if their fruits do multiply,
if the plants from seedlings grow,
and if the clouds their rain distill,
all must come from His right hand,
and never will the arm that tills,
nor the rains that feed the earth,
nor the warmth that wakes the seeds,
have the power to make plants live
if Providence has not decreed
that they have life: all nature's green,
her verdant soul, is His design.

AMERICA

And if all this is as you say,
is He, tell me, so benign,
this God of yours, your Deity,
so kind that he will tolerate
that I touch Him with my hands,
like the Idol I create
from many seeds and from the blood

inocente, que vertida
es sólo para este efecto?

RELIGIÓN

Aunque su Esencia Divina
es invisible e inmensa,
como Aquésta está ya unida
a nuestra Naturaleza,
tan Humana se avecina
a nosotros, que permite
que Lo toquen las indignas
manos de los Sacerdotes.

AMÉRICA

Cuanto a aqueso, convenidas
estamos, porque a mi Dios
tan raras, tan exquisitas
no hay nadie a quien se permita
tocarlo, sino a los que
de Sacerdotes Le sirvan;
y no sólo no tocarlo,
mas ni entra en Su Capilla
se permite a los seglares.

CELO

¡Oh reverencia, más digna
de hacerse al Dios verdadero!

OCCIDENTE

Y dime, aunque más me digas:
¿será ese Dios, de materias
como de sangre, que fue
en sacrificio ofrecida,
y semilla, que es sustento?

RELIGIÓN

Ya he dicho que es Su infinita
Majestad, inmaterial;
mas Su Humanidad bendita,

of innocents, blood that is shed
for this alone, this one intent?

RELIGION

Although in Essence the Godhead
is both invisible and vast,
as that Essence is combined
And with our Being bound so fast,
thus He is like to Humankind,
and His benevolence allows
that undeserving though they be,
He may be touched by hands of Priests.

AMERICA

In this much, then, we are agreed.
For of my God the same is true,
and none may touch our Deity
except for those who as His priests
to serve Him have authority;
not only may He not be touched,
but neither may they enter in
His Chapel who are not ordained.

ZEAL

What reverence, whose origin
were better found in Our True God!

OCCIDENT

Then tell me, though much more you swear:
is this God formed of elements
that are as exquisite, as rare,
as that of blood shed valiantly
and offered up as sacrifice,
as well as seeds, our sustenance?

RELIGION

His Majesty, I say this twice
is infinite and without form,
but His divine Humanity,

puesta incrüenta en el Santo
Sacrificio de la Misa,
en cándidos accidentes,
se vale de las semillas
del trigo, el cual se convierte
en Su Carne y Sangre misma;
y Su Sangre, que en el Cáliz
está, es Sangre que ofrecida
en el Ara de la Cruz,
inocente, pura y limpia,
fue la Redención del Mundo.

AMÉRICA

Ya que esas tan inauditas
cosas quiera yo creer,
¿será esa Deidad que pintas,
tan amorosa, que quiera
ofrecérseme en comida,
como Aquésta que yo adoro?

RELIGIÓN

Sí, pues Su Sabiduría,
para ese fin solamente,
entre los hombres habita.

AMÉRICA

¿Y no veré yo a ese Dios,
para quedar convencida,

OCCIDENTE

y para que de una vez
de mi tema me desista?

RELIGIÓN

Sí, verás, como te laves
en la fuente cristalina
del Bautismo.

found in the Sacrament of Mass,
with mercy, not with cruelty,
assuming the white innocence
which in the seeds of wheat resides,
becomes incarnate in these seeds,
in Flesh and Blood is deified;
here in this Chalice is His Blood,
the Blood He sacrificed for us,
which on the Altar of the Cross,
unsullied, pure, in righteousness,
was the Redemption of the World.

AMERICA

I stand in awe of all you say,
and hearing, I want to believe;
but could this God that you portray
be so loving that as food
He would give Himself to me,
like the God that I adore?

RELIGION

Yes, for in His Wisdom, He
came down with only this in view,
to live on earth among mankind.

AMERICA

So, may I not see this God,
that true persuasion I may find?

OCCIDENT

And I as well, thus will it be
that my obsession be forgot?

RELIGION

Oh, you will see, once you are washed
in the crystalline, holy font
of Baptism.

OCCIDENTE

                    Ya yo sé
que antes que llegue a la rica
mesa, tengo de lavarme,
que así es mi costumbre antigua.

CELO

No es aquése el lavatorio
que tus manchas necesitan.

OCCIDENTE

¿Pues cuál?

RELIGIÓN

                    El de un Sacramento
que con virtud de aguas vivas
te limpie de tus pecados.

AMÉRICA

Como me das las noticias
tan por mayor, no te acabo
de entender; y así, querría
recibirlas por extenso,
pues ya inspiración divina
me mueve a querer saberlas.

OCCIDENTE

Y yo; y más, saber la vida
y muerte de ese gran Dios
que estar en el Pan afirmas.

RELIGIÓN

Pues vamos. Que en una idea
metafórica, vestida
de retóricos colores,
representable a tu vista,
te la mostraré; que ya
conozco que tú te inclinas
a objetos visibles, más

OCCIDENT

        Yes, this I know,
before aspiring to come near
the fruitful table, I must bathe;
that ancient rite is practiced here.

ZEAL

That bathing for your rituals
will not cleanse you of your stains.

OCCIDENT

What bathing will?

RELIGION

            The Sacrament,
which in pure waters like the rains
will cleanse you of your every sin.

AMERICA

The magnitude of this you bring
as notices, as yet I cannot
comprehend, of everything
I would know more, and in detail,
for I am moved by powers divine,
inspired to know all you can tell.

OCCIDENT

An even greater thirst is mine,
I would know of the Life and Death
of this great God found in the Bread.

RELIGION

That we shall do. I shall give you
a metaphor, an idea clad
in rhetoric of many colors
and fully visible to view,
this shall I show you, now I know
that you are given to imbue
with meaning what is visible;

que a lo que la Fe te avisa
por el oído; y así,
es preciso que te sirvas
de los ojos, para que
por ellos la Fe recibas.

OCCIDENTE

Así es; que más quiero verlo,
que no que tú me lo digas.

Escena V

RELIGIÓN

Vamos, pues.

CELO   Religión, dime:
¿en qué forma determinas
representar los Misterios?

RELIGIÓN

De un Auto en la alegoría,
quiero mostrarlos visibles,
para que quede instruída
ella, y todo el Occidente,
de lo que ya solicita
saber.

CELO

        ¿ Y cómo intitulas
el Auto que alegorizas?

RELIGIÓN

Divino Narciso, porque
si aquesta infeliz tenía
un Ídolo, que adoraba,
de tan extrañas divisas,
en quien pretendió el demonio,
de la Sacra Eucaristía
fingir el alto Misterio,

it is now clear you value less
what Faith conveys unto your ears,
thus it is better you assess
what you can see, and with your eyes
accept the lessons She conveys.

OCCIDENT

Yes, it is so, for I would see,
and not rely on what you say.

Scene V

RELIGION

Let us begin.

ZEAL
                    Religion, speak,
to represent the Mysteries,
what form do you plan to employ?

RELIGION

An allegory it will be,
the better to instruct the two,
an *Auto* that will clearly show
America and Occident
all that they now beg to know.

ZEAL

This Allegory as *Auto*,
what title for it do you plan?

RELIGION

Divine Narcissus, for although
America, unhappy land,
adored an Idol symbolized
by signs of such complexity
that through that Idol Satan tried
to feign the highest Mystery,
that of the Sacred Eucharist,

sepa que también había
entre otros Gentiles, señas
de tan alta Maravilla.

CELO

¿Y dónde se representa?

RELIGIÓN

En la coronada Villa
de Madrid, que es de la Fe
el Centro, y la Regia Silla
de sus Católicos Reyes,
a quien debieron las Indias
las luces del Evangelio
que en el Occidente brillan.

CELO

¿Pues no ves la impropiedad
de que en Méjico se escriba
y en Madrid se represente?

RELIGIÓN

¿Pues es cosa nunca vista
que se haga una cosa en una
parte, porque en otra sirva?
Demás de que el escribirlo
no fue idea antojadiza,
sino debida obediencia
que aun a lo imposible aspira.
Con que su obra, aunque sea
rústica y poco pulida,
de la obediencia es efecto,
no parto de la osadía.

CELO

Pues dime, Religión, ya
que a eso le diste salida,
¿cómo salvas la objeción
de que introduces las Indias,
y a Madrid quieres llevarlas?

there was, as well, intelligence
among the Gentiles of this land
of other marvelous events.

ZEAL

And where will they enact your play?

RELIGION

In Madrid, the Royal Town,
the Center of our Holy Faith,
the Jewel in the Royal Crown,
the Seat of Catholic Kings and Queens
through whom the Indies have been sent
the blessing of Evangel Light
that shines throughout the Occident.

ZEAL

But does it not seem ill-advised
that what you write in Mexico
be represented in Madrid?

RELIGION

Oh, tell me, did you never know
an object fashioned in one place
and subsequently used elsewhere?
As for the act of writing it,
you find no whim or fancy there,
but only due obedience
attempting the impossible.
Therefore this work, though it may be
inelegant, its lustre dull,
is owing to obedience,
and not born of effrontery.

ZEAL

Religion, tell me, as the play
is your responsibility,
how do you counter the complaint
that in the Indies was begun
what you would carry to Madrid?

RELIGIÓN

Como aquesto sólo mira
a celebrar el Misterio,
y aquestas introducidas
personas no son más que
unos abstractos, que pintan
lo que se intenta decir,
no habrá cosa que desdiga,
aunque las lleve a Madrid:
que a especies intelectivas
ni habrá distancias que estorben
ni mares que les impidan.

CELO

Siendo así, a los Reales Pies,
en quien Dos Mundos se cifran,
pidamos perdón prostrados;

RELIGIÓN

y a su Reina esclarecida

AMÉRICA

cuyas soberanas plantas
besan humildes las Indias;

CELO

a sus Supremos Consejos;

RELIGIÓN

a las Damas, que iluminan
su Hemisferio;

AMÉRICA

a sus Ingenios,
a quien humilde suplica
el mío, que le perdonen
el querer con toscas líneas
describir tanto Misterio.

RELIGION

The drama's purpose is but one,
to celebrate the Mystery,
as to the persons introduced,
they are but an abstraction,
symbolic figures who educe
the implication of the work,
and no part need be qualified
though it be taken to Madrid;
for men of reason realize
there is no distance that deters,
nor seas that interchange efface.

ZEAL

Prostrate, at the Royal Feet
that regally Two Worlds embrace,
we seek permission to proceed,

RELIGION

and of the Queen, our Sovereign,

AMERICA

at whose feet the Indies kneel
to pledge obeisance once again,

ZEAL

and of her Supreme Councillers,

RELIGION

and Ladies, who illuminate
the Hemisphere;

AMERICA

                and the Erudite
whom I most humbly supplicate
to pardon the poor lack of wit
in wishing with these clumsy lines
to treat so great a Mystery.

OCCIDENTE

¡Vamos, que ya mi agonía
quiere ver cómo es el Dios
que me han de dar en comida,

(*Cantan la* AMÉRICA *y el* OCCIDENTE *y el* CELO)

diciendo que ya
conocen las Indias
al que es Verdadero
Dios de laś Semillas!
        Y en lágrimas tiernas
que el gozo destila,
repitan alegres
con voces festivas:

TODOS

¡Dichoso el día
que conocí al gran Dios de las Semillas!

(*Éntranse bailando y cantando*)

OCCIDENT

My agony is exquisite,
come, show me how in bread and wine
this God gives of Himself to me.

(AMERICA, OCCIDENT, *and* ZEAL *sing*)

Now are the Indies
all agreed,
there is but One
True God of Seeds!
    With tender tears
by joy distilled,
raise voices high
with gladness filled:

ALL

Blessed the day
I came to know the great God of the Seeds!

(*All exit, dancing and singing*)

Fragmento del monólogo de Doña Leonor
en Los empeños de una casa

Si de mis sucesos quieres
escuchar los tristes casos
con que ostentan mis desdichas
lo poderoso y lo vario,
escucha, por si consigo
que divirtiendo tu agrado,
lo que fue trabajo propio
sirva de ajeno descanso,
o porque en el desahogo
hallen mis tristes cuidados
a la pena de sentirlos
el alivio de contarlos.
　　Yo nací noble, éste fue
de mi mal el primer paso,
que no es pequeña desdicha
nacer noble un desdichado;
que aunque la nobleza sea
joya de precio tan alto,
es alhaja que en un triste
sólo sirve de embarazo;
porque estando en un sujeto
repugnan como contrarios,
entre plebeyas desdichas
haber respetos honrados.
　　Decirte que nací hermosa
presumo que es excusado,
pues lo atestiguan tus ojos
y lo prueban mis trabajos.
Sólo diré . . . Aquí quisiera
no ser yo quien lo relato,
pues en callarlo o decirlo
dos inconvenientes hallo:
porque si digo que fui
celebrada por milagro
de discreción, me desmiente

Fragment of Doña Leonor's monologue from
The Trials of a Noble House

If of my life you wish to hear
examples of adversity
in which misfortune manifests
its fury and variety,
then listen, and should I succeed
in adding slightly to your pleasure,
the catalogue of my travail
will entertain you in your leisure,
or, perhaps, as it is purged,
all my wretchedness may find
that though the living causes pain,
the telling creates peace of mind.
    I was born of noble blood,
this was the first of fortune's blows:
good fortune does not accompany birth
as any troubled noble knows,
and though few doubt that noble blood
is fortune's gift, a priceless jewel,
to one who suffers, such a gem
may seem, instead, an obstacle:
how inconsistent in one person,
battling in contradiction,
amid plebian misery,
deference and veneration.
    To tell you I was born with beauty
will be forgiven, I presume,
this truth is witnessed by your eyes
and proved as well by misfortune.
I merely state, I did not wish
to be the one to tell this tale,
in telling or in keeping still
two difficulties I detail:
if I say that I was known
and celebrated for discretion,
I prove the very opposite

la necedad del contarlo;
y si lo callo, no informo
de mí, y en un mismo caso
me desmiento si lo afirmo,
y lo ignoras si lo callo.
Pero es preciso al informe
que de mis sucesos hago
(aunque pase la modestia
la vergüenza de contarlo)
para que entiendas la historia,
presuponer asentado
que mi discreción la causa
fue principal de mi daño.
      Inclinéme a los estudios
desde mis primeros años
con tan ardientes desvelos,
con tan ansiosos cuidados,
que reduje a tiempo breve
fatigas de mucho espacio.
Conmuté el tiempo, industriosa
a lo intenso del trabajo,
de modo que en breve tiempo
era el admirable blanco
de todas las atenciones,
de tal modo, que llegaron
a venerar como infuso
lo que fue adquirido lauro.
Era de mi patria toda
el objeto venerado
de aquellas adoraciones
que forma el común aplauso;
y como lo que decía
fuese bueno o fuese malo,
ni el rostro lo deslucía,
ni lo desairaba el garbo,
llegó la superstición
popular a empeño tanto,
que ya adoraban deidad

by the folly of narration;
but if silent, none will know
the truth of me; you see the question,
in silence, you are uninformed,
in speaking, I betray discretion.
But if in making this account
I must record each incident
(though in so doing, modesty
surrenders to embarrassment)
in order that you understand,
you may with confidence assume
that my discretion clearly was
the foremost reason for my doom.

  Such was my eagerness to learn,
from my earliest inclination,
that studying far into the night,
and with most eager application,
I accomplished in a briefer span
the weary toil of long endeavor,
with diligence, commuting time
through the fervor of my labor;
within a very little time
I was the target of all eyes,
admired, the center of attention,
so immoderately eulogized
that laurels won through industry
were glorified as gifts of God.
I was, through all my native land,
recipient of praise and laud,
the quality of veneration
formed by communal acclaim;
and as the things that all were saying,
to good purpose, or in vain,
by elegance of face and bearing
were not in any way gainsaid,
too soon, a general superstition
was so insistent and widespread
that the idol they'd created

el ídolo que formaron.
Voló la fama parlera,
discurrió reinos extraños,
y en la distancia segura
acreditó informes falsos.
La pasión se puso anteojos
de tan engañosos grados,
que a mis moderadas prendas
agrandaban los tamaños. . . .
　　Entre estos aplausos yo,
con la atención zozobrando
entre tanta muchedumbre,
sin hallar seguro blanco,
no acertaba a amar alguno
viéndome amada de tantos. . . .

now the people deified.
To foreign lands, to distant realms,
Fame spread the tidings far and wide,
and the persuasion distance lends
gave credence to these false reports.
Then Fervor, wearing spectacles
whose lens reality distorts,
saw talents of most modest worth
disproportionately magnified. . . .
    Amid such unrestrained applause
my least reflection stultified,
in all the throng I could not find
for my regard a worthy mark;
and so, belovéd of so many,
I took not one into my heart. . . .

Notes

The standard text of Sor Juana's works is the four volume *Obras completas de Sor Juana Inés de la Cruz* (México: Fondo de Cultura Económica, 1951, 1952, 1955, 1957). The first three volumes were edited by Alfonso Méndez Plancarte; at his death the fourth volume was completed by Alberto G. Salceda. Spanish versions of Sor Juana's poems, and the numbers assigned to them, are taken from this source. It should be noted that Sor Juana did not title her poems; they were added by her editors.

Romances

(1) Méndez Plancarte suggests that Sor Juana's "haste in copying" the poems was due to the pressures of getting them into the hands of the Marquesa de la Laguna in time for a new edition of poems published the year following *Inundación Castálida*.

(48) "en-Tarquin": is a verb invented by Sor Juana—broadly, "to turn woman into man." Her choice of model, however, must be ironic, since Lucretia's rape by Sextus, son of Tarquinius Superbus, is considered to be the cause of Tarquin's deposition.

That Sor Juana could not be a woman "who would serve a man" as wife could be interpreted either as a reference to her state as a nun or as a disinclination to be subservient to a man. The following quartet seems more explicit: "I know only that my body,/ not to either state inclined,/ is neuter, abstract, guardian/ of only what my Soul consigns."

The reference to Aristides, and the following lines with their allusions to envy, echo long passages in the "Respuesta" and lines from Doña Leonor's monologue in *Los empeños de una casa*.

Redondillas

(93) Sor Juana calls Leonor the *Coco*, "the boogeyman." The pun in Spanish is with *coco*, "the coconut palm." The species is changed in English for the sake of a pun.

(94) This is admittedly an *imitation*, not a *translation*.

(95) This is the only instance in which Sor Juana aludes to her bastardy. Octavio Paz finds it remarkable that the accent is more on the question of her father's social rank than of her own legitimacy.

Décimas

(126) This poem lends substance to the conjecture that Sor Juana was an accomplished artist. One of her portraits is believed to be a self-portrait—or a painting copied from a self-portrait—but there are no extant attributed paintings.

(130) Lysi and Fili are names by which Sor Juana alluded to the Marquesa de la Laguna.

Sonnets

(161) Méndez Plancarte laments these "naughty, even gross," exercises, considering them to be indecorous and unworthy of Sor Juana. In explanation, he points out that "one must remember the times." Although her near-

contemporaries Góngora and Quevedo and Lope far surpassed Sor Juana in grossness, it is true that the modern reader is surprised by the earthiness of this and the accompanying four sonnets for which Sor Juana was asked to fit a poem to prescribed end-rhymes. Is it possible that Sor Juana could not refuse the challenge of the game?

Silva

(216) Written in hepta- and hendecasyllabic lines alternating without pattern, and with cross rhyme, the English version substitutes lines of pentameter for the long, eleven-syllable Spanish lines, and for the Spanish seven-syllable lines, freely varying lines of dimeter, trimeter, and tetrameter. This pattern allows for maximum flexibility in English while maintaining some resemblance to the original—the most flexible of Spanish classic forms. The rhyme imitates the freedom of the Spanish cross-rhymed form.

Paz considers this to be Sor Juana's most personal poem, "poetry of the intellect confronting the cosmos." The poem recounts the voyage of the soul in its quest for knowing. Mendez Plancarte includes a helpful prosification in his notes to the poem.

Villancicos

(317) Méndez Plancarte believes that the allusion to the surrender of the "Prudent Men" inevitably recalls Sor Juana's own triumph over the celebrated Portuguese priest Antonio de Vieyra; it was, nonetheless, a costly triumph, leading, as it did, directly to the confrontation of the "Respuesta."

Sor Juana's argument that women should "argue, tutor, learn" is a major theme of the "Respuesta."

Méndez Plancarte points out that Catherine was the patron saint of the "Royal and Pontifical University of Mexico." As Sor Juana was denied any connection with that body, I suspect that the saint's patronage was of much less interest to her than what she symbolized.

There is an ironic and tragic foreshadowing in the lines "now all her learned arguments/ are lost to us. . . ." We do have four volumes of Sor Juana's writing, but her personal papers, as well as additional literary and intellectual works, have been lost.

Theater

(367) A loa was a brief theatrical work which could be performed in isolation but more frequently preceded an auto [sacramental play] or comedia [profane or non-religious work].

The allusion to the Mexican's origins in the sun, according to Méndez Plancarte, was reported by Friar Andrés de Olmos: "The Sun cast down an arrow . . . and made a hole, from which a man emerged . . . and, following, woman . . ."

The "God of the Seeds" might refer to several Aztec gods, but here is most obviously Huitzilopochtli, the most powerful of the gods of Tenochtitlán, the Aztec capital built on the site now occupied by central Mexico City. Méndez Plancarte quotes early sources recounting the rites devoted to the seed god: "They [the Indians] each year concocted the figure of Huitzilupuchtli . . . of various edible grains and seeds. . . . They ground them to form the said statue, of the size and stature of a man. The liquid with which they bound and mixed the flour was the blood of children. . . . After a month's time . . . they took a dagger . . . and struck the Idol in the breast. . . . They said that they killed the God Huitzilopuchtli in order to eat of his body . . . and they divided it in very small portions among all those of their *barrios* . . . and this was their manner of Communion . . . and they called this food *Teocualo*, which means *God is eaten*."

AMERICA's lines, "what value precious ores untold/ if their excrescences befoul/ and sterilize a fertile earth. . ." are surely the earliest recorded comment in this continent of environmental concerns.

Scene II

AMERICA's protest to Zeal, calling him a "mad, blind, barbaric man" who was "disturbing our serenity," is very daring, considering that ZEAL is the enforcer of the Faith.

The last lines of the scene authentically illustrate the Indians' awe before the weapons of the Spanish, especially firearms and the horse.

Scene IV

This scene is particularly interesting. In it, Sor Juana accurately describes the synonymies between the pre-Columbian and the Catholic religions: the benificence of the Gods (rather exaggerated, considering Huitzilopochtli's true characteristics), the inviolability of the Gods; the cleanliness practiced in their worship; the Gods' blood sacrifice; and the ritual of the Mass. Paz discusses this Jesuitical syncretic vision at length in his *Sor Juana Inés de la Cruz* . . . and the vision is underlined in Sor Juana's quotation from Paul, arguing that all along, although unknowingly, the Indians had been worshipping the True God.

Scene V

This final scene is Sor Juana's apology and apologia. At the same time it provides a resolution—"Now are the Indies/ all agreed,/ there is but One/ True God of Seeds!"—that removes any possibility of criticism from her earlier defense of the customs and practices of indigenous New Spain.

(388) This fragment from Doña Leonor's monologue in *Los empeños de una casa* [The Trials of a Noble House] is generally conceded to be autobiographical. With the exception of her "noble birth," Leonor does indeed seem to represent Sor Juana's not overly modest but entirely objective vision of herself.